"Oh...It's like CSI..."

A Qualitative Study of Job Satisfaction Experiences of Forensic Scientists

Tharinia Dukes-Robinson

and

Ashraf Esmail

University Press of America,® Inc.
Lanham · Boulder · New York · Toronto · Plymouth, UK

Copyright © 2014 by
University Press of America,® Inc.
4501 Forbes Boulevard
Suite 200
Lanham, Maryland 20706
UPA Acquisitions Department (301) 459-3366

10 Thornbury Road
Plymouth PL6 7PP
United Kingdom

All rights reserved

British Library Cataloging in Publication Information Available

Library of Congress Control Number: 2013954245
ISBN: 978-0-7618-6284-0 (paperback :   paper)
eISBN: 978-0-7618-6285-7

We would like to dedicate this book to all diligent forensic scientists. They have a passion for forensic science and not only continue to advance the field but also ensure that fellow forensic scientists and the field as a whole maintain and follow the highest quality, integrity, and ethical standards available.

CONTENTS

Table	viii
Preface	ix
Foreword	xi
Acknowledgments	xiii
Chapter One. Introduction	1
Introduction to the Problem	1
Background of the Study	3
Statement of the Problem	4
Purpose of the Study	6
Research Question	7
Significance of the Study	7
Definition of Terms	7
Assumptions and Limitations	8
Nature of the Study	9
Theoretical/Conceptual Framework	10
Previous Methodologies Used to Measure Job Satisfaction	11
Theory Guiding the Study	12
Organization of the Remainder of the Study	14
Chapter Two. Literature Review	15
Introduction	15
Relevant Literature	16
Overview of Stress in Law Enforcement	16
Overview of Job Satisfaction in Law Enforcement	21
Forensic Science and Forensic Scientists	24
Job Satisfaction and Forensic Personnel	26

The Current Study	27
Summary	28
Chapter Three. Methodology	29
Introduction	29
Theoretical Framework	30
Research Design	30
Sample Design	31
Measures	33
Field Testing	34
Data Collection Procedures	35
Data Analysis Procedures	36
Limitations of Methodology and Strategies for Minimizing Impact	37
Credibility	37
Transferability	38
Expected Findings	38
Ethical Issues	38
Conclusion	39
Chapter Four. Data Collection and Analysis	41
Introduction	41
The Researcher	42
Participants' Demographics	42
Interview Guide Questions	44
Participants' Profiles	45
Data Collection	47
Data Analysis	49
Data Clustering and Thematizing	49
Research Findings	50
Theme One: Comparison to Forensics on TV	50
Theme Two: Unrealistic Expectations From Others	51
Theme Three: *CSI* Effect Hinders Job	53
Theme Four: Job is Satisfying	54
Theme Five: Work Affects Lives of Others	55
Major Findings	56
The Research Question	57
Goals of the Interview Questions	57
Summary	59
Chapter Five. Results, Conclusions, and Recommendations	61
Introduction	61
The Research Question	61
Summary of the Theoretical Perspective	62
Summary of Results	64
Conclusions as Related to the Literature	64
Limitations of the Study	66
Significance of the Study	68
Implications and Future Recommendations	69

Future Recommendations	70
References	73
Index	81
About the Authors	83

TABLE

Table 4.1: Participant (P) Demographics　　　　　　　　　43

PREFACE

With the emergence and popularity of television series such as *CSI, Criminal Minds* and *Law & Order*, interest in forensics as academic field of study and career choice has blossomed. This blossoming is, in part, due to the glamorization of the profession and its employees. These media portrayals, however, do not address the stress, workload, and interpersonal interaction issues that accompany most professions—including forensic science. As a response to the shallow and fictionalized accounts of forensic science and scientists' occupations offered by the media, this study provides a much needed dose of reality.

Using face-to-face interviews with forensic scientists who work in crime laboratory settings, Dukes and Esmail reveal the real story behind being a forensic scientist and one's satisfaction with on the job experiences. They interviewed both male and female forensic scientists, aged 25 to 54 years, and whose experience in the profession ranged from two to thirty-two years. The scientists on-the-job specialties covered a variety of tasks, from controlled substances, firearms, and biology tests to DNA analysis. Their academic training consisted of bachelors and masters of science degrees in the areas of Criminalistics, Biology, Chemistry, and Biochemistry.

In revealing the real story about forensic science and job satisfaction, Dukes and Esmail address multiple objectives. First, they seek to discover what types of responsibilities are associated with the forensic science occupation. Second, they compare these real life responsibilities to those displayed in the media. Third, they investigate how these fictitious portrayals affect forensic science and the criminal justice process. Fourth, they examine how factors such as pay, work pace, technology, interpersonal interaction, and providing help to others associated with the profession impact forensic scientists' job satisfaction.

Like their fictitious counterparts in television shows, the forensic scientists in real life are highly satisfied with their jobs and do enjoy providing assistance to victims, the community, and society. However, the real life scientists are irritated by the falsehoods about their occupations presented in the media. Not every case investigated is quickly and clearly resolved. Not every case can be resolved with just a "touch" of DNA. Others employed in law enforcement and court-related occupations, as well as jurors in court cases, often do not have a clear understanding of what is possible for a forensic scientist to accomplish; often the forensic scientists encounter others in their interactions whose understandings have been influenced by the media (known as the "*CSI* Effect"). This means that the scientists must spend extra time and energy re-educating others about their occupations, while at the same time performing their normal job tasks.

While no one publication alone can reduce the "*CSI* Effect" on public perceptions about forensic science as a occupation or what falsehoods are perpetuated in the media for the sake of entertainment, this book does make an important contribution in the direction. By revealing the similarities and discrepancies between the real and fictitious lives of forensic scientists, perhaps this book can serve as another source of re-education for others about forensic work.

Lisa A. Eargle, Ph.D.
Francis Marion University

FOREWORD

Job satisfaction is very important in forensic science because it is the very scientific means whereby those in the field gather evidence to solve very complex cases. The research conducted by Dr. Tharinia S. Dukes and Dr. Ashraf Esmail seems to support the aforementioned. They are aware of the importance of evidence based on research and they believe that their book cuts into the heart and soul of what forensic scientists and students should be knowledgeable about.

As has been indicated in the past, there must be a connection between the text and the students. In their research and writing Drs. Dukes and Esmail unmistakingly seek to explain the very essence of current issues in the field of a growing and dynamic academic topic.

In order to fully realize the optimal job satisfaction, it is imperative that educators in this very important academic core be able to prepare students in a manner that will allow them to reach their fullest potentials. Therefore, competency for students must be at the forefront of this unique learning experience. Drs. Dukes and Esmail certainly have given profound thought to the subject matter at hand. Their hard work and dedication to this area of concentration are both meaningful and timely.

As a criminologist and criminal justician, I am keenly aware of the many books and research related to forensic science. Moreover, unique and thoughtful writing and ideas are known to fill a void in the field. The authors of this book have done this and even more.

> Dr. John Penny
> Chair
> Social Sciences Department
> Southern University at New Orleans

ACKNOWLEDGMENTS

We would like to express our heartfelt appreciation to the devoted forensic scientists who gave their valuable time to assist us in this study. These eight extraordinary individuals' willingness to accommodate the authors in this groundbreaking study was unparalleled. The forensic scientists' participation not only aided this study by contributing to the criminal justice and forensic science knowledge base but it also offers those outside the field of forensic science the opportunity to gain a true understanding of what it means to work as a "real" forensic scientist. The insight that these professionals provided exposed what those of us in the field already know: that forensic science and forensic scientists are not "as seen on TV." If it were not for these hardworking individuals this book would not have been possible.

CHAPTER ONE
INTRODUCTION

INTRODUCTION TO THE PROBLEM

As demonstrated by the barrage of television shows and other media, forensic science has never been more popular. The field has not seen such an interest in forensics since the 1970s when television shows such as *Quincy, MD* thrust forensics into the spotlight. In the 1980s interest in forensics seemed to dwindle. However, in the 1990s with the breakthrough of DNA analysis, forensic science once again became one of the most popular fields of study and work. Today forensic shows such as the *CSI* and *Law & Order* franchises have sensationalized forensic science and one of its key players, forensic scientists. These shows often depict forensic scientists as laid back, well dressed, stress free super crime fighters who experience enormous job satisfaction (Bassett, 2006; Kruse, 2010; Ramsland, 2009). This glamorization of the forensic scientist has become such a phenomenon that it has begun to impact university curriculums (National Institute of Justice, 2007; Stankiewicz, 2007).

Forensic science curriculums are rapidly being added to university academic agendas across the country as well as abroad. However, a vast majority of these programs lack standardized academic curriculums and are producing graduates who are improperly trained (Desio, Gaensslen & Lee, 1985; National Institute of Justice, 2007; Sykes, Holland, & Shaler; 2006). According to the Council on Forensic Science Education, a great number of students are completing these substandard programs and finding that when they seek employment at crime labs and other law enforcement agencies the agencies are not impressed by the curriculum completed (Council on Forensic Science Education, n.d.; National Institute of Justice, 2007). Recognizing that there is a shortfall in forensic education, forensic science organizations such as the American Academy of Forensic Sciences (AAFS) have been expeditiously assisting universities with their curriculums to ensure quality forensic education is being provided (FBI Law Enforcement Bulletin, 2007; Jones, 2009).

American Academy of Forensic Sciences and other reputable forensic science organizations employ committees that use evaluation and accrediting processes to improve university curriculums (Jones, 2009; National Institute of Justice, 2007). With the help of such consortiums, universities have improved their curriculums and are providing accredited forensic science education programs that will meet the needs of potential students. These improved forensics curriculums will also meet the demand of a workforce seeking qualified individuals who are educationally and not television trained in forensics (National Institute of Justice, 2007; Stankiewicz, 2007). Additionally, strengthening and continuing to add forensic education to the academic curriculum will also minimize the valuable time and expense it costs forensic agencies to train new hires (National Institute of Justice, 2007; National Research Council, 2009). It can often take up to two years of training an individual before a single case can be assigned. If an individual receives a forensic education from an accredited forensic science program then an employer, crime laboratory director, or other hiring body can be more assured that a potential applicant meets the job qualifications (Almirall & Furton, 2003; National Institute of Justice, 2007).

Having university accredited forensic science education programs is a great leap in the quest for quality forensic science education. However, what is immediately needed is the institution of professional forensic training centers as well as advanced educational programs in forensic science ("Science in Court", 2010). Just as bachelors and masters level forensic education programs are becoming commonplace in university curriculums, it is with great hope doctoral forensic science programs will have similar results.

With all the media attention given to forensic science due to television shows such as *CSI, Law & Order, Criminal Minds, Cold Case,* and *Court TV,* the public has developed a fascination with forensic science (Dowler, Fleming & Muzzati, 2006; Mann, 2006; Mopas, 2007). The fascination is so great that the shows' creators are having a hard time trying to keep up with demand (Stankiewicz, 2007). These shows commonly depict forensic science, forensic scientists, and the evidence recovered as flawless. These shows also conclude every week with the forensic team always "catching the bad guy". These depictions are somewhat misleading because it gives the nonprofessional the impression that forensic science is infallible and that forensic scientists are glamorous, stress-free, super crime fighters (Bassett, 2006; Minn, 2009; Ramsland, 2009). Often, as with media portrayals, these views are unrealistic when it comes to how crime and the justice system interact (Bassett, 2006; Dowler, Fleming & Muzzati, 2006; Ramsland, 2009; Toobin, 2007). Real issues, such as the potential stress and poor job satisfaction the forensic scientist may experience in their day-to-day quest to solve crime, often do not find their way into the storyline. One reason may be that such things may not capture and retain the attention of the viewers. What many entering the field quickly discover is that forensic science and forensic scientists are not "as seen on TV."

The primary duty of the forensic scientist in a crime laboratory is to conduct day-to-day analysis of evidence while adhering to very stringent laboratory, bureau, nationally or internationally accreditation guidelines as well as various other organizational requirements. To add even more pressure, the forensic scientist must complete such day-to-day evidence analysis in a timely and accurate manner, ensure chain of custody, maintain strict quality control and data management, write the completed report, and testify in court to the completed analysis just to name a few of many miscellaneous duties (American Academy of Forensic Sciences, 2008; Barbara, 2008). Additional demands forensic scientists often experience with each case include last minute requests for evidence processing, competency and proficiency testing, case backlogs, dealing with investigators or prosecutors, and dealing with many other organizational requirements (California Crime Laboratory Review Task Force, 2009; Houck, 2006; McDonald, 2008; U.S. Department of Justice, 2007). A rigorous load such as this makes working within a crime laboratory anything but glamorous. All of these factors as well as other factors necessary to complete analysis of a case could make for a potentially stressful work environment, which may yield job dissatisfaction.

BACKGROUND OF THE STUDY

The area of police and law enforcement stress and job satisfaction has been the subject of continual research and discussions (Brough & Frame, 2004; Manzoni & Eisner, 2006; Mire, 2005; Sewell, 2000; Wells, 2003). With the success of forensic science shows on television today the image projected of forensic scientists and the job is a very entertaining one. The image often presented is that solving crime takes nothing more than the forensic scientist effortlessly collecting evidence and having high-tech instrumentation yield immediate results. Frequently such imagery perpetuates misconceptions of the job real forensic scientists perform.

Forensic scientists and forensic laboratories are increasingly under pressure to yield rapid, superior, and inexpensive forensic services (Becker & Dale, 2007; Mannell & Shaw, 2006). Forensic scientists and their labs are expected to meet many extraneous demands. These individuals and their organizations must also maintain high ethical standards and integrity set by the individual laboratories, the American Society of Crime Laboratory Directors (ASCLD), the International Organization for Standardization (ISO), or other forensic accrediting bodies they wish to be affiliated. Meeting demands for excellence compounded by the increase in evidence submission (often line police officers cannot discern what evidence is or is not important so they often submit everything found at the scene) to crime laboratories has created backlogs in many laboratories across the country (McDonald, 2008; Murphy, 2007; National Institute of Justice, 2007; Rincon, 2005). In fact, according to Lyons (2006), the recognized backlogs are greatest when it comes to DNA and many state crime laboratories are unable to keep up with the requests for analyses. These demands are not only causing case backlogs in forensic laboratories across the United States but are also placing forensic scientists in potentially stressful work environments. Similar to any other type of work environment a negative, work environment in the crime laboratory setting could potentially lead to job dissatisfaction among the crime laboratory's forensic scientists.

STATEMENT OF THE PROBLEM

According to one of the executive producers of the television show *CSI*, shows like *CSI* do create misunderstandings as to the capabilities of forensic science and forensic scientists but at the same time, such shows demonstrate how forensics can be a powerful tool in solving crimes (Sappenfield & Goodale 2003). The reality is that crime laboratories in this country are often understaffed, lack the latest technology, operate out of antiquated facilities, and are often forced to operate on meager annual budgets ("*CSI* Experts Showcase", 2007; Houck, 2006; Sewell, 2000). Furthermore, trying to schedule casework around court dates, dealing with investigators and attorneys, meeting organizational and accreditation protocol, or even dealing with individuals who actually believe that forensic scientists can solve a case in 24 hours or less, are only a few more of the many daily challenges encountered by forensic scientists (Sappenfield & Goodale 2003). Having to efficiently and effectively deal with so many variables when it comes to forensic science casework can be exceedingly stressful and can make the job less satisfying. Regardless, it is extremely important for forensic scientists to be alert because the bottom line is that the results of their analysis have an impact on a suspect or victim's life.

Pressure within any type of work environment could lead to poor job satisfaction amongst employees. With respect to forensic scientists, dealing with the many types of pressures or stressors experienced on a daily basis that comes with the job of crime solving could yield low job satisfaction. Research and literature on job stress and job satisfaction among law enforcement has been significantly researched and discussed for many years. As Sewell (2000) points out, "academicians, researchers, and practitioners have critically examined subsets of the law enforcement population, including executives and administrators, investigators, officers with unique responsibilities, and non-sworn personnel such as dispatchers" (p. 1).

Some of the Sewell's (2000) subsets, as discussed above, have been extensively studied by researchers such as Castle in 2008 (jail officers), Burke in 1995 (dispatcher stress), and collaboratively by Childress, Talucci, and Wood in 1999 (correctional officers). There are countless other researchers and subset areas that have been profoundly researched with respect to law enforcement be it stress, satisfaction, attitudes, and so on. However, one area that still seems to be under-researched and not mentioned in the peer-reviewed literature is that of job stress, job satisfaction or any other potential variables that affect forensic personnel. In fact, the entire forensic science field as a whole is significantly under-researched. A recent detailed report on the current state of forensic science in the United States released by the National Research Council (2009) sites a number of concerns in forensic science that needs to be addressed to ensure the discipline's future a success. One of the concerns listed in this report includes the fact that forensic science suffers from the lack of an adequate research base compared to other disciplines (National Research Council, 2009).

Except for defining what a forensic scientist or forensic personnel is or is not, literature related to any attitudes, feelings or behavior of forensic personnel is relatively sparse. A few non-peer reviewed articles on forensic technician or crime scene responder stress were located but the articles did not reflect that any type of in-depth research in the topic area had been conducted. Additionally, dissertation work in the area of forensic science personnel stress or job satisfaction was sparse. While conducting this research, only two dissertations focusing on forensic personnel were located. The first dissertation partially focused on traumatic stress of forensic technicians in Israel and the information was later published in a traumatic stress journal (Hyman, 2004) while the second dissertation's focus was on dispatcher stress (Burke, 1991). An extensive review of the literature gives the appearance that the current trend or focus of the bulk of forensic science research, dissertations, and articles centers around the coined term *CSI* Effect. The term *CSI* Effect is used to describe the ideology that due to all the television shows such as *CSI*, *Law & Order,* and other similar media the public acquires an unrealistic expectation of forensic science and its capabilities (Mann, 2006; Willing, 2004). The concern with the *CSI* Effect literature is how the "*CSI*" phenomena affect the science or business of forensic science. What is often not addressed in the *CSI* Effect literature is how the rapidly expanding field of forensic science is affecting the forensic scientist and other forensic personnel mentally and physically. This further demonstrates that the recent report released by the National Research Council (NRC, 2009) is correct in that forensic science research is indeed lacking compared to other law enforcement entities.

There was modest success in locating research on the effects of the nature of forensic science work on specific forensic personnel, laboratory directors. Research on this specific forensic personnel, laboratory directors, was located in the Federal Bureau of Investigation's literature archives of *Forensic Science Communications.* In that April 2000 issue of *Forensic Science Communications,* James Sewell investigated stress among forensic laboratory managers. Sewell's investigation effectively pointed out all the stressors that are placed on forensic laboratory managers and what can be done to mitigate some if not all stressors that come along with the job of forensic laboratory manager. What this particular piece of literature demonstrated to this researcher is that there is growing awareness of the impact that the rapidly expanding field of forensic science is having on all forensic personnel.

Though there are articles that are often presented as feature topics in some news magazines, there appears to be no existing research that examines stress and job satisfaction among forensic scientists. The review of the literature on various other law enforcement personnel stress and job satisfaction experiences assisted in identifying that indeed there is a gap that exists on forensic scientist and forensic personnel stress, job satisfaction, and other pertinent issues that could potentially affect the job of conducting forensic work.

Forensic science personnel (dispatcher, scientist, crime scene responders, and others) is an area that is in need of research. The primary way that organizations can effectively address the needs of its forensic personnel is to learn how to identify and deal with any potential issues that may arise. Research or literature specific to forensic personnel could provide forensic organizations with the ability to recognize and address issues its forensic scientists may be experiencing. Prominent researcher Sewell's (2000) review of the law enforcement literature confirmed that there indeed is a need for further research of psychological, physiological, and other manifestations of forensic science personnel distress that are often overlooked by management.

This study's primary goal was to provide information that will assist crime laboratories and other law enforcement entities to understand some of the issues its forensic scientists may potentially experience. A secondary goal of this study was to stimulate research in the forensic sciences with respect to forensic science personnel and symptoms they may encounter such as job satisfaction, stress, and other psychological and physiological issues.

PURPOSE OF THE STUDY

The purpose of this study was to examine how forensic scientists experience the role of job satisfaction in their daily employment setting. A phenomenological approach allowed the study to explore job satisfaction experiences among forensic scientists by asking questions about daily work setting experiences. The resultant research from the study will add information to the rather scant amount of data related to the variable job satisfaction when it comes to forensic scientists, thus filling the existing gap in the literature.

RATIONALE

The rationale for this study was to explore whether real-life forensic scientists experience high job satisfaction. Currently, there is a perception held by many outside the field that the work of a forensic scientist is glamorous, exciting, and not as stressful compared to some other professions (Sykes, Holland, & Shaler, 2006; Ramsland, 2009; Schweitzer & Saks; 2007; Warrington, 2008). The reality is that forensic scientists encounter a number of challenges, such as dealing with outside pressures from law enforcement and attorneys, organizational expectations, staffing issues, and the like that make the job of solving crime a very difficult task (Houck, 2006; Warrington, 2008). Because of such challenges, forensic scientists may be experiencing less job satisfaction than is perceived.

RESEARCH QUESTION

As Neuman states (2003), many people get their ideologies about crime and other related things from television, movies, or print media, which is not the social reality of how things really are. The focal point of this research was to explore job satisfaction experiences among forensic scientists by asking questions about daily work setting experiences. The study examined the lived experiences of forensic scientists to answer the following question: *How do forensic scientists' daily employment setting experiences play a role in job satisfaction?*

SIGNIFICANCE OF THE STUDY

This study used basic qualitative methodology to describe the Participants' perception of their experiences with job satisfaction working as forensic scientists. The information obtained from this research will contribute to the gap in the forensic science literature in the area of job satisfaction as it relates to forensic scientists. Furthermore, the results obtained could be utilized by forensic organizations as a reference tool to investigate job satisfaction. It is anticipated that this research will stimulate future research interest in the area of forensic scientist job satisfaction, forensic scientist stress, and all other potential occupational issues for which forensic scientists may most likely be susceptible. Acknowledgment of job aspects that potentially cause poor job satisfaction among forensic scientists could be used by organizations to minimize or eliminate negative aspects of the job, such as the prevention of case errors and burnout. Moreover, identifying aspects of the job that forensic scientists are dissatisfied with could assist forensic science organizations in assessing how or what can be done to improve poor job satisfaction in the workplace.

DEFINITION OF TERMS

This phenomenology study often used terminology that may not be understood by individuals who are not familiar with the field of forensic science. Some of the terms that may need an explanation are defined within this brief section.

AAFS: American Academy of Forensic Sciences (AAFS) is a professional organization that provides guidance to advance the application of science to the law and whose objective is to promote education, research and encourage teamwork in the forensic sciences (American Academy of Forensic Sciences, 2008).

Acute Stress: Acute stress is experienced when an imagined or real threat is immediately perceived by an individual. The imagined or real threat immediately perceived can be physical, psychological, or emotional (Scott, 2005).

ASCLD: American Society of Crime Laboratory Directors (ASCLD) is a professional organization that consists of crime laboratory directors and forensic science managers dedicated to fostering excellence in the forensic sciences (ASCLD.org, n.d).

Chain of Custody: This process refers to the written record (containing dates, reasons, and so on) of persons who have contact with evidence from the point of inception until the evidence's final disposition (Rush, 2000).

Crime scene: A place, person or object that becomes subject to a criminal investigation (Millen, 2000).

Criminalist: A name or title used by some law enforcement agencies to describe a person who applies science to the law to assist the legal system in solving crime.

Chronic Stress: Stress that results from constant demands and pressures for extended periods of time; stress that occurs over a long period of time; person sees the situation as a miserable one with no hope or no way out and gives up trying to find a solution (American Psychological Association, 2011; Torpy, Lynm, & Glass, 2007).

CSI Effect: The term *CSI* Effect is used to describe the ideology that due to all the television shows such as *CSI, Law & Order,* and other similar media the public acquires an unrealistic expectation of forensic science and its capabilities (Mann, 2006; Willing, 2004).

Forensic science: Forensic science is the application of science to assist the law or legal profession in solving crime.

Forensic scientist: A forensic scientist is a person who applies science to the law to assist the legal system in solving crime.

Investigation: An investigation is the "process of search and examination to discover facts" (Millen, 2000).

ISO: International Organization for Standardization (ISO) is the organization that develops and publishes international standards (International Organization for Standardization, 2009).

Job Satisfaction: Refers to how satisfied an individual is about his or her job; the degree to which a person likes or dislikes his job; employee's positive and negative feedback about how content they are with the job ("Job Satisfaction", 2011; Spector, 1997).

Stress: Physical or emotional factors that cause physical or mental tension on an individual ("Stress", 2009).

ASSUMPTIONS AND LIMITATIONS

According to Leedy and Ormrod (2005), assumptions are the expectations of the researcher that are often taken for granted. This study assumed the following:
- It was assumed that the Participants would be receptive to the study.
- It was assumed that the Participants would be forthright in their interviews.

Some limiting factors that were beyond the control of the researcher and could have potentially influenced the results of the study and how the results were interpreted include:
- Due to the small number of forensic scientists interviewed, the results could not be generalized to all other agencies or forensic scientists.
- Forensic scientists not being honest with their answers could have produced results that were inaccurate.
- Due to daily time constraints and heavy work caseloads, forensic scientists could have been rapid in their responses and not give the interview time serious attention, as they could possibly be more concerned with getting back to work.
- Some Participants could have had second thoughts about participating in the study and thus may not have been as forthright with responses.
- There could have been underlying factors that contribute to the forensic scientists' job satisfaction other than the factors associated with the job.

As mentioned above as the primary limitation, this qualitative study could have been potentially limited due to a small sample size and the fact that all the forensic scientists happen to be employed by the same crime laboratory. As such, this study cannot be generalizable to all forensic scientists.

NATURE OF THE STUDY

According to Leedy and Ormrod (2005), qualitative research focuses on phenomena that occur in the real world. This study observed the true nature of forensic scientist work and investigated whether the job has the high or significant satisfaction as perceived by those who think they know what forensic work entails. This basic qualitative research approach employed the methodology of one-on-one interviews. One-on-one interviews allowed more control over the line of questioning (Creswell, 2003). Employing an interview methodology was the best fit for this study because it allowed a more personal rapport with each Participant. Developing a personal rapport was important because it assisted in getting a better understanding of the forensic scientists' job satisfaction because the Participants felt more at ease to speak freely (Creswell, 2003; Leedy & Ormrod, 2005). Open-ended, semi-structured questions from the Forensic Scientist Experiences Interview Guide were used to collect information on job satisfaction experiences among selected forensic scientists.

According to Sproull (2002), an open-ended response format has several advantages. One advantage to using the open-ended response format is that such a format will elicit information that is original (Sproull, 2002). Another advantage is the opportunity for the Participant to give opinions or add comments that are personal to them (Sproull, 2002). Lastly, when existing information on a given topic is limited, using an open-ended response format can potentially add new information (Sproull, 2002). Thus, the open-ended response format was ideal for this study because there was very little information on forensic scientists and job satisfaction and any information that resulted from this study would be a contribution to the forensic science and criminal justice community.

THEORETICAL/CONCEPTUAL FRAMEWORK

Phenomenology is a philosophical movement that was pioneered by German philosopher Edmund Husserl (Aspers, 2004; Moustakas, 1994). According to Moustakas (1994), Husserl defined phenomenology as "the 'science of science' since it alone investigates that which all other sciences simply take for granted or ignore, the very essence of their own subjects" (p. 46). Phenomenology's focus is to observe Participants experiencing a phenomenon and then describe the commonalities experienced by the Participants (Creswell, 2003). There are two approaches that phenomenology can take when trying to understand the phenomena or experiences of individuals, descriptive and interpretive.

Husserl and his ideas have been credited with the formation of the descriptive phenomenological approach (Flood, 2010). The descriptive phenomenological approach is an inquiry method that requires the researcher to interact with the subjects being studied. The descriptive approach also requires that the researcher investigate the phenomena or lived experience without bias as well as without interjecting his beliefs about what is happening with the individuals or phenomena being studied (Wojnar & Swanson, 2007). In other words, this approach is concerned with how everyday life events affect the individual.

The second approach to phenomenology is the interpretive phenomenological approach. The interpretive phenomenological approach suggests that the focus of the investigation be on the lived experiences of the individuals and allows the researcher and Participants to bring preconceived ideology into the process to assist with explaining the phenomena (Flood, 2010; Wojnar & Swanson, 2007). In other words, interpretive phenomenology is interested in how individuals function or manage their daily lives or place in the world. Descriptive phenomenology was the theoretical prospective used to support this study's methodology.

The underlying basis of this research was to understand and describe phenomena from the Participant's point of view (Creswell, 2003; Leedy & Ormrod, 2005; Mertens, 2005). For this basic qualitative study, phenomenological methods were used to collect and analyze data as well as interpret the findings. The descriptive phenomenology method was the ideal approach to take for this study because this approach allowed the researcher to gather Participants' perceptions or meaning of a specific experience or phenomena (Mertens, 2005). Additionally, this methodology allowed the researcher to learn how individuals function in their daily lives and to better understand the lived experiences of individuals being studied (Creswell, 2003; Neuman, 2003). In other words, this qualitative approach allowed the researcher to gain a better understanding of how forensic scientists function on a daily basis. Most importantly, this approach allowed the researcher to gather perspectives as to how these daily duties contribute to job satisfaction or dissatisfaction.

PREVIOUS METHODOLOGIES USED TO MEASURE JOB SATISFACTION

According to Landy (1978), Edwin Locke described job satisfaction as "a pleasurable or positive emotional state resulting from the appraisal of one's job or job experiences" (p. 533). An individual's attitude about the job or job experiences comes from a variety of factors as hierarchical as organizational and managerial to factors as minute as coworker interactions. For many years, demographic characteristics of job satisfaction, such as gender, age, and number of years on the job have been the focus of research in many job genres. To measure the multitude of factors that influence job satisfaction, both quantitative and qualitative methodologies have proven successful over the years (Bhushan, 2005; Rode, 2005; Spector, 1997).

Quantitative research methodologies typically provide the researcher or organization with methods such as surveys, questionnaires, longitudinal, cross-sectional, experimental, or quasi-experimental options for which to gauge employee satisfaction. Equally, qualitative research methodologies also provide the researcher or organizations several avenues to measure job satisfaction. However, qualitative methodologies utilize methods such as interviews, focus groups, or case studies to capture the Participant's lived experiences of job satisfaction. Review of previous job satisfaction literature, law enforcement and non-law enforcement, have demonstrated that when it comes to job satisfaction no matter what employment field or demographic explored, quantitative as well as qualitative methodologies have been successfully utilized to measure job satisfaction (Gurbuz, 2007; Kirk-Brown & Wallace, 2004; Kleck, Tark, & Bellows, 2006; Perron & Hiltz, 2006; Pietersen, 2005; Rode, 2005; Spector, 1985).

No matter what employment genre, a plethora of literature on job satisfaction can be found. However, the same cannot be said about job satisfaction in law enforcement. Boke and Nalla (2009) conducted an extensive review of the literature and found that law enforcement job satisfaction research is sparse compared to other employment areas. Though sparse, the Boke and Nalla research did locate quantitative literature on job satisfaction of police, corrections, probation, and so forth that utilized information-gathering techniques such as surveys, questionnaires, and other quantitative methods. The existence of quantitative literature, with regard to job satisfaction in the various law enforcement entities, can be reviewed in the peer-reviewed works of many prominent researchers (Boke & Nalla, 2009; Brough & Frame, 2004; Castle, 2008; Manzoni & Eisner, 2006; Miller, Mire, & Kim, 2009; Zhao, 2002) in law enforcement. By the same token, qualitative research literature using methods such as interviews, field studies, and other direct observations as it relates to law enforcement job satisfaction is also sparse but does exist (Sims, Ruiz, Weaver, & Harvey, 2005; Write & Bonnett, 2007).

This current study's review of the literature found that sub-specialties of law enforcement, particularly forensic science, suffer from a severe lack of research base in quantitative as well as qualitative research (National Research Center, 2009; Sewell, 2000). Based on literature review of law enforcement studies using various methodologies to research job satisfaction, it appeared that there has been success using quantitative as well as qualitative methodologies. This was a good indicator that perhaps this current study could find success using qualitative methodologies since forensic science is a sub-specialty field of law enforcement.

This research employed the methodology that was the most appropriate or best fit to complete the study. There are many methods commonly used to study criminal justice topics. Kleck, Tark, and Bellows (2006) conducted research to determine exactly which methods where the most used to study criminal justice and criminology topics. Their research found that of the quantitative methodology, survey research was the most popular method of acquiring criminal justice information followed by cross-sectional experimental designs, and multivariate statistical methods (Kleck, Tark, & Bellows, 2006). For qualitative methodology, Kleck et al. (2006) found that the primary methods used for criminal justice and criminology research inquiries used interviews and direct observation. For this qualitative study, the interview method was employed. For this criminal justice sub-specialty, forensic science, conducting interviews was perhaps the most appropriate method to answer the research question as it related to job satisfaction experiences of forensic scientists.

THEORY GUIDING THE STUDY

A review of the literature revealed a number of theorists who have formulated theories to explain why people have the attitudes that they do when it comes to their jobs. Three of the more prominent theorists to explain job satisfaction include Edwin Locke, Edward Lawler, and Frank Landy. Edwin Locke in 1976 and Edward Lawler in 1973 devised the discrepancy theory to explain job satisfaction and Frank Landy in 1978 devised the opponent process theory to explain job satisfaction. After reviewing the literature associated with the three prominent theories, as well as other theories and theorists, Landy's opponent process theory appeared to be the best fit to observe if job satisfaction changed over time even though the core duties of the job had not. Landy's opponent process theory was the theory guiding this phenomenology study.

DISCREPANCY THEORY: EDWIN LOCKE AND EDWARD LAWLER

In 1976, Edwin Locke developed the discrepancy theory to explain an individual's job satisfaction. According to Locke's (as cited in Dunnette, 1976) theory, job satisfaction involves needs and is determined by a discrepancy of what one would like in a job versus what one currently has in a job (Bhushan, 2005; Pietersen, 2005). As such, any satisfaction or dissatisfaction of certain aspects of the job will depend on how the individual's perceptions or needs are of the aspect of the job at the time of inquiry. Basically, if an individual feels that he did not get or is not getting what he expects out of a job he will be dissatisfied with the job (Gurbuz, 2007).

Another prominent theorist to explain job satisfaction was Edward Lawler in 1973. Lawler used Locke's theory as a framework to formulate his version of discrepancy theory, which is slightly opposite of Locke's theory. Lawler's version of discrepancy theory posits discrepancy is the "result of the difference between an actual outcome a person received and some other expected outcome level" (Castillo & Cano, 2004, p. 65). Simply put, Lawler believes that job satisfaction results when the individual gets what he feels he deserves and what he expected out of the job. This theory is widely used to explain pay and job satisfaction (Castillo & Cano, 2004; Lee, Phelps, & Beto, 2009).

OPPONENT PROCESS THEORY: FRANK LANDY

Landy was another prominent theorist to use theory to explain job satisfaction. Landy, in 1978, developed his opponent process theory to explain how satisfied an individual is with a job over time. Opponent process theory was first proposed by Solomon and Corbit in 1973 to aid in their study of human emotions in their work with skydivers. The theory posits, "any motivational stimulus activates two opposing processes" (Vargas-Perez, Tin-A-Kee, Heinmiller, Sturgess, & van der Kooy, 2007, p. 3713). With the initial process, the onset is fast and ends simultaneously as the stimulus whereas the second process not only opposes the first processes action but also starts and ends slowly and lasts longer than the stimulus (Vargas-Perez et al., 2007). What this process translates into is that people are in a state of "hedonic neutrality" meaning that on average, people are viewed as being relatively stable or at equilibrium (Bowling, Beehr, Wagner, & Libkuman, 2005).

Although Solomon and Corbit in 1973 developed the theory to assist in their research with the emotion of skydivers, many theorists have used the theory to explain phenomena or as a theoretical framework for their own opponent process theory. Because it has been applied successfully in many different research areas, opponent process theory may be generalized to an area such as job satisfaction (Bowling et al., 2005). In 1978, Frank Landy used Solomon and Corbit's 1973 opponent process theory philosophy to formulate his opponent process theory of job satisfaction.

According to Landy's further explanation of Solomon and Corbit's opponent process theory, all emotional or pleasure states experienced by people tend to follow a regular pattern of change. That pattern of change, when it comes to emotional behavior, is as follows:
- An external stimulus excites the individual.
- Once the stimulus excites the individual to critical levels an opposing inhibitory process begins and brings the excitement back to normal or to an acceptable range.
- The external stimulus and the opponent process disappears (Landy, 1978).

Landy uses the Solomon and Corbit opponent process theory's pattern of change to suggest that when it comes to the job, regardless of the work environment people seem to show a stable or constant level of job satisfaction (Landy, 1978). In other words, even though over time a job may not change, the satisfaction that one gets from the job does change (Bhushan, 2005). Landy's 1978 version of opponent process theory best fit this study in that it supported the researcher's hypothesis that the job of forensic scientist may not have an excessively high or significant job satisfaction experience as those outside the field perceive and that satisfaction may change over time.

OPPONENT PROCESS THEORY AND THE CURRENT STUDY

Using Landy's opponent process theory as theoretical support, this research sought to examine job satisfaction of forensic scientists. The desired result was data that would support the hypothesis that the job of forensic scientist does not have the high job satisfaction as often depicted or perceived and will fall in line with the opponent process theory that guided this study. If the data produced proved successful, this study would demonstrate that similar to other jobs, satisfaction with ones job as a forensic scientist changes over time.

ORGANIZATION OF THE REMAINDER OF THE STUDY

The remainder of the dissertation is organized as follows: Chapter Two briefly discusses relevant literature on stress in law enforcement, job satisfaction within law enforcement, forensic science and forensic scientists, and concludes with the goals of the current study. Chapter Three discusses research methodology, research questions, population sample, instrumentation, data collection procedures, and data analysis. Chapter Four presents the results and findings of the data analyses. Lastly, Chapter Five will discuss results, conclusions, implications and recommendations for future research.

CHAPTER TWO
LITERATURE REVIEW

INTRODUCTION

The purpose of this chapter was to briefly discuss relevant research on the two very distinctive areas of stress and job satisfaction within law enforcement, the field of forensic science, and forensic scientists. The chapter concludes with a discussion of what the current study expected to demonstrate.

There was limited research directly related to forensic science personnel, job satisfaction, or job stress. The literature review process involved extensive research on other areas of law enforcement with regard to job satisfaction and job stress. This research was conducted to demonstrate that due to the nature of the job it is possible that forensic personnel also experience similar issues as such law enforcement personnel as police, probation, corrections, and the like.

The literature review contained research that was retrieved from various sources including but not limited to professional peer reviewed articles and forensic science, criminal justice, and law enforcement journals, books, databases (such as UMI ProQuest Criminal Justice journal, Academic Search Premier, Science Direct), and psychological and sociological journals just to name a few. A common theme observed from the review of the literature was that although modern law enforcement personnel may be experiencing job dissatisfaction, literature or research on the topic was relatively non-existent except for short peer-reviewed articles on the subject. There was a plethora of information on law enforcement personnel (such as police, corrections, probation) as it related to stress but minimal information on law enforcement personnel as well as forensic personnel job satisfaction. Review of the literature revealed that there is definitely a need for continued research in the area of forensic science personnel as it relates to stress, job satisfaction, and many other potential job related concerns associated with forensic science personnel.

Relevant Literature

Many factors contribute to how an individual views his work environment. Factors such as attitude towards management, coworker interaction, scheduling is often considered when gathering feedback from employees regarding the work environment (American Psychological Association, 2007). Two of the more common factors repeated by employees when evaluating the employee and work environment relationship are stress and job dissatisfaction ("Stress," 2008; American Psychological Association Media Room, 2007; Castillo & Cano, 2004). Although, stress and job satisfaction are two distinct components, they are often viewed as one unit because of the somewhat symbiotic relationship that exists (Manzoni & Eisner, 2006). One possible reason for this one unit idea could be some preconceived notion that if an employee is stressed at the job then that employee will be dissatisfied with the job. Thus, the notion that stress creates job dissatisfaction. However, that thought may not necessarily hold true.

A recent American Psychological Association (2007) study reports that one-third of residents surveyed in the U. S. reported that they experience extreme stress levels and one in five states that they experience stress about 15 days or more per month. Furthermore, according to the American Psychological Association (2007), when it comes to specific types of jobs stress levels and number of days experienced are more likely to be higher due to the nature of the job. This is a factual assessment that can be applied to many areas of law enforcement related employment. As society continues to grow and become more complex, enforcing the law also continues to grow and become more complex. Due to this complexity, it should be every law enforcement organization's goal to provide a workplace environment that contains minimal stress to ensure job satisfaction among its employees (Boke & Nalla, 2009; Brody, DeMarco & Lovrich, 2002; Brough & Frame, 2004). Perhaps this goal is something all organizations strive for but more often than not keeping stressful environments to a minimum may not always be possible.

Stress in law enforcement is not a new subject of discussion. Enforcing the law in American society has never been an easy job and over the past few decades, it has become a job that faces great challenges. Television shows may paint a picture of law enforcement as effortless as well as glamorous but the reality is that the profession is for the most part opposite of that commonly held view (Caudill, 2008; Finneran, 2003; Postrel, 2007). These shows often portray unrealistic case solving abilities, rapid case solving, yet rarely show the amount of stress or low job satisfaction law enforcement personnel experience.

Overview of Stress in Law Enforcement

Research conducted by organizations such as the National Institute for Occupational Safety & Health (NIOSH) and the National Women's Health Resource

Center (NWHRC) report that 40 percent of workers report their jobs as being tremendously stressful ("Stress," 2008; National Institute for Occupational Safety & Health, 1999; National Women's Health Resource Center, 2002). The same research also found that 25 percent listed their jobs as the number one stressor in their lives (National Institute for Occupational Safety & Health, 1999; National Women's Health Resource Center, 2002). Left untreated, stress in the workplace cannot only lead to workplace injury but can also lead to serious health problems such as cardiovascular disease and psychological disorders (National Institute for Occupational Safety & Health, 1999; Sheehan & Van Hasselt, 2003). With stress having the ability to cause so much havoc on the body physically as well as psychologically, it is pertinent that employers work to not only prevent workplace stress but also have in place policies to effectively deal with employee stress once it is acknowledged.

Stress is by all account a normal part of life and is necessary to maintain balance. However, according to Finn (1997) and Varhol (2000) when stress hinders an individual's ability to function in life and becomes abnormal or a problem stress should be immediately addressed. Moreover, it is often difficult to determine what is or is not a stressful event because what may be considered stressful to one individual could be considered non-stressful to another individual. Because of this inability to characterize what a stressful event is or is not, defining stress can be challenging. What makes defining stress challenging is that there really is no standardized conformity as to what stress is (Harpold & Feemster, 2002; Stinchcomb, 2004). As such, the term stress has slightly varied definitions depending on the context or subject matter in which it is being referenced.

A simplified definition of stress provided by Webster's dictionary defines stress as any "physical, mental, or emotional strain that is caused by anxiety or overwork" ("Stress", 2005, p. 1426). Other literature reviewed gave definitions of stress using verbose and often more technical explanations than the simple aforementioned Webster's definition. To further support the complexity of defining stress, a National Institute for Occupational Safety & Health (1999) study suggests the causes of job stress, the effects of job stress, and how to prevent job stress still remains somewhat perplexing, which is what makes it difficult to define stress. Again, this goes back to the ideology that stress cannot be generalized from person to person but must be addressed more on an individualized basis (Finn, 1997; Harpold & Feemster, 2002; Stinchcomb, 2004; Varhol, 2000). Therefore, determining exactly which situations on the job are most stressful can be an arduous task.

Regardless of which definition of stress one selects, the overall understanding is that stress is very detrimental to an individual's physical and mental well-being. Over the past few decades, the employment industry has taken serious notice on the subject of stress in the workplace, stress on productivity, and has sought ways to reduce workplace stress (National Institute for Occupational Safety & Health, 2009; Santa-Barbara & Shain, 1999; Zhao, He, & Lovrich, 2002). As a result, research on job stress has grown tremendously over the past few decades, especially in law enforcement.

According to Kenny and Cooper (2003), the call for research in the field of law enforcement over the past few decades has been a result of societal as well as workplace changes. Employment in the field of law enforcement demands mental as well as physical rigor. Over time, such demands coupled with other factors such as organizational, managerial, personal, and other pressures can cause serious stress to develop within the law enforcement employee (National Institute of Justice, 2007; Sewell, 2006; Sheehan & Van Hasselt, 2003). The type and severity of the stress varies depending on the individual, how the individual handles stressful situations, and other factors that collectively bring about a stress episode. A few generic signs of stress include:

- Fatigue
- Anxiety
- Head and muscle aches
- Weight loss or gain
- Depression
- Shortness of breath
- Chest pain or pounding chest
- Irritability, anger or mood swings (Mayo Clinic, 2007, National Institute for Occupational Safety and Health, 1999a; National Institute for Occupational Safety and Health, 1999b; National Women's Health Resource Center, 2002).

These are by no means the only indicators of stress. As stated earlier, there exists a variety of definitions of what defines stress or what stress entails.

It should be noted that another difficulty with determining whether an individual is experiencing stress is the fact that stress symptoms often imitate the symptoms of other problems the individual may have (APA, 2007; Mayo Clinic, 2007; National Women's Health Resource Center, 2002). For example, chest pain or pounding chest could perhaps be a sign of a heart condition or some other condition unrelated to work or life stressors.

As previously discussed, determining signs and symptoms of stress is complex. Insert underlying health problems that mimic signs of stress and the complexity of identifying stress become even greater. This is why it is important that claims of stress be viewed on an individual or case-by-case basis. Just because an entire population does not view the situation as stressful does not necessarily mean that a stressful situation does not exist. With a profession such as law enforcement, it is critical that any signs of stressful situations or stressors be immediately recognized and effectively addressed (Brough, 2004; Castle, 2008; Childress, Talucci, & Wood, 1999).

One might ask why is the focus of stress such an important issue in the field of law enforcement. Due to the nature of the law enforcement field and its various entities, one can expect that stress will be present in some form. The issue of stress is significant for the reason that not only does potential stress affect the law enforcement professional experiencing it but this stress also has the potential to affect the people these professionals serve. For example, law enforcement personnel taking out their frustrations on citizens, making mistakes that affect innocent citizens, and other negative law enforcement and public interactions may result because of a stressed law enforcement personnel (Sewell, 2006; Stinchcomb, 2004). Moreover, a stressed law enforcement personnel may also produce a dissatisfied law enforcement personnel. This is not good for employee or organization moral and could rapidly become a major problem for an organization. Hence, it is imperative that organizations do the best that they can to prevent as well as alleviate unnecessary stress in its law enforcement personnel.

According to Finn (1997), some of the factors that contribute to the ideology that law enforcement has become an extremely dangerous profession go as far back as the early 1980s to late 1990s when violent crime, fear of contracting blood borne and airborne diseases, public scrutiny, and many other social and economical problems were at an all time high. Policing during this violent period of the criminal justice system was already difficult then to add social and health risk concerns seriously overwhelmed the patrol officer (Finn, 1997). When such concerns or stressors become excessive to the point that it affects job functioning, job satisfaction, and other areas of the law enforcement personnel's job and life, stress becomes a serious issue. Enforcing the law, which is already a dangerous job, becomes even more dangerous because you now have a stressed out officer on the streets.

As noted earlier, the effect that stress has on law enforcement personnel is a topic area that has been profoundly researched throughout the years. Much of the early literature on police stress emerged during the early 1970s (Burke, 1995; O'Connor, 2006; White, Lawrence, Biggerstaff & Grubb, 1985). Correctional officer, probation officer, and other law enforcement personnel have also been the focus of many stress studies. These areas of law enforcement are growing and becoming more interconnected within the law enforcement culture and experience stress similar to the traditional law enforcement sector (Brough, 2004; Childress, Talucci & Wood, 1999; Curran, 2003; Finn, 1997; Gillan, 2001; Harpold & Feemster, 2002; National Institute of Justice, 2007; Richardson, Burke, & Martinussen, 2006; Sewell, 2006; Sheehan & Van Hasselt, 2003; Wells, 2003). Recent research has also expanded to include the effects of stress and even job dissatisfaction on law enforcement support staff such as dispatchers, technicians, and scene responders. The results of these studies demonstrate that indeed law enforcement personnel, regardless in what area or capacity, because of the nature of their jobs, have the potential to and are experiencing great amounts of stress as well as poor job satisfaction (Burke, 1995; U. S. Department of Health & Human Services, 2007).

As demonstrated by the vast amount of available research viewed in the area of law enforcement job stress and satisfaction, it appears that there has been a steady increase throughout the years of stress and job dissatisfaction in law enforcement personnel. One reason for this increase may be due to the high and sometimes unrealistic expectations and demands from the public, management, courts and the like have become everyday factors in the law enforcement personnel's daily routine (Doak & Assimakopoulos, 2006; National Institute of Justice, 2007; Sewell, 2000; Stinchcomb, 2004). Policing has become without a doubt more multifaceted than in years past. As the criminal justice system continues to adapt to accommodate an ever-changing society, changing technology, changes in the types of crime and individuals entering the system, policing will also continue to adapt. This intricacy in policing has also brought to the job stressors that reflect the changing times.

According to Sewell (2006), stress within society and modern organizations is a very serious problem. Stressors such as career concerns, abnormal work hours, working environment, and undefined or unclear work roles are a few concerns that organizations cannot ignore. Law enforcement agencies must take great efforts to minimize stressors in order to preserve not only the welfare of the organization but also the welfare of its law enforcement personnel and subsequently the welfare of the public that they protect and serve (National Institute for Occupational Safety and Health, 1999; National Women's Health Resource Center, 2002; Stinchcomb, 2005). It cannot be reiterated enough that it is of great importance that law enforcement employers immediately take action to prevent stress in the workplace. Additionally, it is necessary that law enforcement employers have the skills to recognize the signs of an employee having stress or job satisfaction related issues and immediately address such issues. One possible way law enforcement organizations can prevent or diminish stress and job dissatisfaction in the workplace is by seriously examining the extensive research in these two areas and take immediate action when either or both is suspected.

The information available to law enforcement organizations from research can and has been used by law enforcement to assist in not only identifying stress in their employees but also offer ways in which to diminish or avoid stress. For instance, many organizations today offer a variety of programs to assist employees deal with stress in the workplace as well as personal stressors outside of work that the employee may be experiencing (Garcia, Nesbary, & Gu, 2004; Harpold & Feemster, 2002; Sewell, 2006; Sheehan & Van Hasselt, 2003; Wells, 2003). However, according to the National Institute for Occupational Safety and Health (1999), in order for these stress programs to be successful in their stress reducing or preventing efforts organizations must be sufficiently prepared and follow these three steps: problem identification, intervention, and evaluation.

One way organizations can address problem identification, intervention, and evaluation would be through the establishment of stress reduction programs (National Institute of Justice, 2007). Though employers recognize the usefulness of stress reduction programs to their employees, there is some concern that stress reduction programs may be costly to the organization. While these programs may take away from an organization's overall budget, the alternative could prove more costly. For instance, employees going out on stress claims, excessive sick days, resigning from the job and other psychological or physiological issues can prove more costly to an organization than providing stress related programs (Wells, 2003). Not providing stress reduction programs to law enforcement personnel could lead to stressed personnel making major or costly mistakes that are not only disadvantageous to the law enforcement personnel but also could lead to loss of life, litigation, and other liabilities for the organization (Brough, 2004; Childress et al, 1999; Finn, 1997).

Unhealthy working environments combined with personal issues such as family, health, and other psychological and physiological issues are potential stressors law enforcement personnel are exposed to and must cope with. These professionals must deal with such issues all while trying to enforce the law and live up to the expectations of the modern law enforcement profession. The fact that law enforcement organizations are acknowledging and assisting with psychological and physiological stressors of its personnel is a step in the right direction to guarantee the safety of its employees. It is also a step in the right direction to maintaining employee job satisfaction in this often involved profession.

OVERVIEW OF JOB SATISFACTION IN LAW ENFORCEMENT

Perhaps one of most widely used definitions of job satisfaction was coined by Edwin Locke. According to Edwin Locke (as cited in Dunnette, 1976), job satisfaction is a positive emotional state that is the result of an individual's appraisal about their job or the job experiences (Miller, Mire & Kim, 2009; Saari & Judge, 2004). When an individual experiences stress symptoms singularly or in combination, it can create a complex work environment for both the employer and employee. Three of the more prevalent symptoms that have been associated with workplace stress include burnout, poor concentration, decreased productivity, and job dissatisfaction (Kohan & O'Connor, 2002; White, Lawrence, Biggerstaff, & Grubb, 1985). Organizations recognize the costly effects of burnout, loss of productivity, and other types of stress that could lead to job dissatisfaction and thus recognize the importance of job satisfaction to the organizational well-being.

In the law enforcement field, when these symptoms (burnout, loss of productivity, and other types of stress) find their way into the workplace, the human and monetary costs could prove detrimental to not only the employee but also the organization's environment and perhaps its existence. The latter of the three prevalent symptoms, lack of job satisfaction, has been one of the newer areas of concern and study in law enforcement in recent years. In fact, within the fields of organizational and industrial psychology, job satisfaction has been one of the most popular variables in history to be studied (Bowling, Beehr, Wanger, & Libkuman, 2005; Miller, Mire & Kim, 2009).

When discussing job stress what also should be considered is the possibility that job dissatisfaction may also exist. Low or poor satisfaction with one's job can be found in many professions. According to Brough and Frame (2004), job satisfaction is routinely explained as an enjoyable experience or state that results from a positive assessment of the job or job experiences. When it comes to jobs, there will always be an employee who is satisfied, moderately satisfied, extremely dissatisfied, or variations within the range of job satisfaction or dissatisfaction. The profession of law enforcement is no exception.

Research in the area of job satisfaction among law enforcement personnel demonstrates that the following are a few reasons given by law enforcement personnel as to why job satisfaction is lacking:

- Inferior supervision
- Unrealistic or unnecessary deadlines
- Heavy caseloads
- Lack of respect or support shown by the organization
- Lack of respect or support shown by immediate management
- Lack of respect or support shown by the public it serves
- Lack of or ineffective communication
- Low pay
- Long and inconsistent hours and work schedules
- Constantly having their actions dissected by management, the organization, public, attorneys (Childress et al, 1999; Dowler, 2005; Sewell, 2006; Sheehan & Van Hasselt, 2003).

According to the literature reviewed, researchers in various areas of the criminal justice field found that members surveyed in corrections, probation, police, and other law enforcement entities consistently gave the aforementioned, as well as numerous others, as reasons for job dissatisfaction (Castle, 2008; Lambert & Hogan, 2009; Manzoni & Eisner, 2006; Sheehan & Van Hasselt, 2003). Law enforcement officials in today's society acknowledge these concerns and primarily focus on diligently reviewing invaluable information on law enforcement stress, job satisfaction, and other related research. Reviewing such literature will definitely aid law enforcement officials in assisting its employees as well as provide a better working environment.

In their research, Manzoni and Eisner (2006) reported that for law enforcement work related stress evolved mostly from job related stress and organizational related stress. Job related stressors have been identified as those factors that law enforcement officers must deal with on an everyday basis as part of the routine duties of the position (Childress et al., 1999; Manzoni & Eisner, 2006; Sewell, 2006). For instance, heavy caseloads, time constraints, dealing with the sometimes not too friendly public and so on are a few common daily tasks that law enforcement personnel experience that can quickly turn into daily stressors. Dealing with such stressors day in and day out could potentially prove detrimental to job satisfaction among the law enforcement personnel.

Organizational stressors have been identified as those factors that mainly are bureaucratic in nature (Brough, 2004; Stinchcomb, 2004). For instance, inferior supervision, lack of management support and so forth are a few common daily tasks that law enforcement personnel experience. Similar to job related stress organizational related stressors affects the law enforcement personnel directly and could rapidly turn into daily stressors and job dissatisfaction. Conversely, Manzoni and

Eisner (2006) point out that though these two particular primary stressors is addressed individually, it is possible for an organizational stressor to elicit acute stress and for a job related stressor to produce a chronic stress response. This somewhat dysfunctional symbiotic relationship demonstrates how organizational and job related stress adversely affects job satisfaction. Consistent with Manzoni and Eisner (2006), other researchers concur that organizational stress is considered the primary cause of stress in the workplace (Greene, 1989; Kohan & O'Connor, 2002). The realization that stress in the workplace starts as high as the organizational level and descends to the routine job level guides modern organizations to strive not only reduce job stressors but also maintain job satisfaction (Greene, 1989; Manzoni & Eisner, 2006).

As briefly covered in the stress section, when discussing job stress, it is inescapable to avoid discussing job satisfaction. If one is stressed on the job, it is most likely they will also not be satisfied with some aspect of or the job as a whole. Similar to job stress discussed previously, level of job satisfaction is very important to an employee and subsequently the employer. An unsatisfied employee may result in an unproductive employee, work errors, unsafe work environment, and so forth that potentially affects the organization as an entity. Earlier research on levels of job satisfaction of police, corrections, and probation officers as well as some other law enforcement personnel has demonstrated that by diminishing stress among police officers job satisfaction improves (Castle, 2008; Dantzker, 1997; Greene, 1989; Mire, 2005). Research further demonstrates that similar to job stress job satisfaction is also a big predictor of such negative workplace variables as:

- High job turnover
- Job burnout
- Absenteeism
- Organizational dissatisfaction
- Managerial or supervisor dissatisfaction
- Coworker dissatisfaction (Castle, 2008; Dowler, 2005; Kohan & O'Connor, 2002; Wright & Bonett, 2007).

Moreover, not unlike job stress job satisfaction has a large impact on not only how law enforcement personnel perceive and carry out their jobs. Similar to job stress, negative attitudes as a result of job dissatisfaction are reflected onto the public that they serve (Brough, 2004; Mire, 2005; National Women's Health Resource Center, 2002).

It is pertinent that law enforcement organizations ensure that its personnel's level of job satisfaction be closely monitored. Any potential issues should be rectified immediately because the ramifications of ignoring the problem could prove devastating to personnel, the organization, and the public. As echoed by Mire (2005), law enforcement organizations should be seriously concerned with how satisfied its personnel are with their job based on four primary reasons:

1. Any negative attitudes personnel may have about the job may unfavorably affect the law enforcement personnel's job performance.

2. Any negative attitudes personnel may have about the job may unfavorably affect the public's attitude or views the public may develop about police and the organization as a whole.
3. Law enforcement organizations have a moral obligation to be concerned about their employees and should foster positive attitudes among the ranks.
4. Research has demonstrated that increased or positive job satisfaction reduces the amount of stress and stressors experienced by law enforcement personnel (Mire, 2005, p. 28).

If law enforcement organizations begin by addressing even one of these four primary issues a more positive or satisfied employee may be the result. This may in turn produce a positive working environment and other positive outcomes that would be beneficial to all connected to the law enforcement personnel.

The field of forensic science has been rapidly expanding and compared to other areas of law enforcement garnering the majority of the limelight the past several years thanks to the barrage of media interest, primarily entertainment television, in the field (Finneran, 2003; Minn, 2009; Robbers, 2008; Willing, 2004). Nonetheless, research in the forensic sciences and its forensic scientists with regard to job satisfaction has not quite reached the same status as job satisfaction research in other areas of law enforcement. The objective of the next section is to provide a brief overview of forensic science and forensic scientists. It is the researcher's expectation that the section will provide some insight into the field of forensic science and the true role of the forensic scientist in the crime solving process.

FORENSIC SCIENCE AND FORENSIC SCIENTISTS

What is forensic science? There are many definitions as to what forensic science entails but the basic definition more commonly used is the application or use of science in law or legal proceedings (American Academy of Forensic Sciences, 2008; Sykes, Holland, & Shaler, 2006). Early instances of the application of science to law, forensic science, have been found to date back to the year 800 B. C. (Rudin & Inman, 2002). Forensic science is not a science that can miraculously deliver rapid responses as to the who, what, where, and why of a crime, which is perhaps the biggest misconception due to the popularity of media forensic science (Finneran, 2003; Ramsland, 2009; Williams, Rickard, & Fisher, 2005). Many know the story of the infamous nineteenth-century fictitious character Sherlock Holmes and his trusty assistant Dr. Watson. As those Sir Arthur Conan Doyle stories were read or viewed as theatrical films or television shows, many were probably not aware that the use of science to solve crime would later be formally known as forensic science. To the avid readers or viewers, Sherlock Holmes was just an entertaining whodunit mystery story and the connection that this was the application of science to the law was probably never given a thought.

In the 1970s, forensic science continued to stimulate interest with television sensation *Quincy, ME* and cop shows like *Dragnet*. Such dramas would routinely highlight burgeoning forensic fields such as latent print or questioned documents.

Today, disciplines like questioned documents and latent prints are highly specialized areas and play a significant role in modern forensic science. Although such media laid the foundation for raising awareness of forensics, many credit the 1990s as being the period where interest in forensic science really saw resurgence. With media favorites such as *NCIS, Law & Order* and *CSI* franchises or forensic based news shows that can be found on *Court TV* or A & E's *Cold Case Files*, just to name a few, forensics has become overwhelmingly popular (Becker & Dale, 2007; Mennell & Shaw, 2006; Robbers, 2008). These shows have practically taken over television and on any given day at any given hour, one can find some type of forensic show or series of forensic shows available for viewing. Although the barrage of current forensic science shows are heavy on the drama and often over-exaggerate forensic science capabilities, a semblance of fact from these shows can often be found or find its way into real forensic science (Becker & Dale, 2007; Campbell, 2007; Goode, 2004).

To illustrate how fictitious forensic science sometimes influence real forensic science it has been said that Edmond Locard, considered the father of trace evidence, credits Sherlock Holmes for the idea that trace evidence such as soil and other small particles can have evidential value (Saferstein, 1982). Modern forensic science as we know it can attribute its origins to outstanding individuals and contributors to the field such as Francis Galton (developed the basic principles of fingerprint classification), Albert S. Osborn (developed the principles of Questioned Documents), and as mentioned earlier Edmond Locard who developed physical evidence techniques and principles (Erzinclioglu, 2004; Hilton, 1993). In fact, it is Locard's exchange principle that is the basic principle for forensic science. Locard's principle simply states that every contact leaves a trace (Erzinclioglu, 2004; Rudin & Inman, 2002; Saferstein, 2004, 1982).

The individuals who work within the field of forensic science analyzing evidence are often referred to as forensic scientists. Depending on the organization, individuals could also be referred to as criminalists, forensic analysts, and by a few other name variations. A forensic scientist is an individual who uses scientific knowledge or applies science to the law to assist law enforcement, attorneys, courts, and others within the legal community (American Academy of Forensic Sciences, 2008). How do these individuals use their scientific knowledge to assist the legal community? Ask a real life forensic scientist and he probably will say with a grin that he does not assist the legal community in the fashion his television counterpart does.

According to shows like *CSI*, forensic science professionals are the crime scene investigator, the analyst, the interrogator, the arresting officer, the case presenter at trial all rolled into one (Sykes, Holland, & Shaler, 2006). The problem with such depictions, according to Dr. Max Houck and other scholars in the field, is that when the show *CSI* airs that not only are laymen watching but police officers and prosecutors are also watching and the amount of evidence that is submitted to forensic laboratories becomes astronomical (Rincon, 2005; Schweitzer & Saks, 2007). Despite the fact that these fictitious shows bring awareness to the field, the majority of the current forensic science shows often present forensic science in a very unrealistic light and the lines between fiction and reality are often blurred (Goode, 2004; Shelton, 2008; Tesler, 2010). If only television forensics were truly reflective of real life forensics.

The reality when it comes to forensic science is that in most major municipalities forensic scientists specialize in one area rather than be generalists in all areas. Perhaps in small town America a forensic scientist or law enforcement official may take on many forensic roles out of necessity and not necessarily to be like *CSI*'s fictitious jack-of-all-trades character Grissom. Another point is that Grissom, Sherlock Holmes and his trusty assistant Dr. Watson, and other fictitious super forensic scientists always tend to not be under any great stress or appear to be unsatisfied with their jobs as crime solvers. However, the same may not be quite true for today's real-life crime solvers. Real forensic scientists not only deal with solving the crime but must also deal with attorneys, courts, victims, offenders, other law enforcement entities, heavy caseloads, and a host of other factors that often does not end simply because the work day has ended (Dowler, 2005; Sewell, 2006; Sheehan & Van Hasselt, 2003).

JOB SATISFACTION AND FORENSIC PERSONNEL

The image often portrayed is that forensic personnel are always available to immediately respond to a scene in record time, have endless resources available or that every forensic organization has every type of state of the art equipment imaginable just to name a few misconceptions (Finneran, 2003; Kruse, 2010; Ramsland, 2009; Schweitzer & Saks; 2007). On the contrary, forensic personnel are often overworked, have limited financial resources available and often work with common everyday or outdated tools rather than the fancy state of the art equipment seen on the popular forensic shows. Moreover, forensic personnel often deal with very real factors such as:

- The pressure that there are zero margin or tolerance for errors
- Massive amounts of evidence being submitted for analysis
- Dealing with demanding investigators and/or prosecutors
- High organizational and managerial expectations
- Being understaffed and overworked (Manzoni & Eisner, 2006; Sewell, 2000, 2006).

As discussed earlier, prominent leaders in the field (Goode; 2004; Houck, 2006; Williams, Rickard, & Fisher, 2005) concur that shows like *CSI, Law & Order, NCIS* and other similar entertainment shows convey the positive aspect of awareness to the field of forensic science. However, these scholars also concur that the negative aspect such shows convey is that of unrealistic expectations of forensic science by law enforcement, attorneys, jurors, and the general public. These high expectations are then placed upon the forensic scientist thus presenting a potentially stressed and dissatisfied forensic scientist. Such negative factors and working environment could have serious effects on the organization, forensic scientist, casework output, and casework results, which ultimately affects a victim's or suspect's life. As Kruse (2010) states, *CSI* forensic science is nothing more than wishful-thinking science.

The pressures and demands placed on the forensic scientist on a daily basis may cause him to experience stress that could lead to job dissatisfaction. Such manifestations could affect the organization's ability to retain the forensic scientist. According to a recent report by the California Crime Laboratory Review Task Force (2009), when it comes to retention of forensic scientists in crime laboratories across the state, some of the main reasons for unhappy forensic scientists include salary, lack of advancement opportunities, and burnout from heavy caseloads. It is important for the law enforcement organization to recognize any stressors the forensic scientist may be experiencing. Once these have been identified, the agency should immediately find ways to minimize or prevent stress in order to maintain or improve job dissatisfaction. Managing dissatisfaction is not only detrimental to the employee's well-being but also detrimental to the well-being of the organization.

THE CURRENT STUDY

Due to the nature of forensic work, it was this study's assumption that forensic scientists experience varying levels of job satisfaction. Variables such as stress, unrealistic expectations, organizational demands, dealing with the courts and other law enforcement agencies, and many other variables play an immense role in the forensic scientist's daily work life. Moreover, various minute and often not thought of daily tasks that are necessary and often arduous add even more pressures for the forensic scientist. For example, when one thinks of forensic scientist, small daily tasks such as making copies, fielding calls on multiple cases, making case folders, returning evidence to agencies and a multitude of other laboratory tasks are not taken into account. Such daily tasks are not the images depicted by the fictional forensic scientists on television. The imagery presented to the public, which is somewhat unrealistic, is that of forensic scientists never getting anything wrong, they are in great physical condition, wear stylish clothes, and are extremely attractive (Goode, 2004; Kruse; 2010; Ramsland, 2009).

What this study did was examine job satisfaction among a small sample of forensic scientists to investigate their forensic scientist job satisfaction experiences. The primary goal of this study was to produce information that would contribute to the wide gap in the literature on forensic science personnel as well as stimulate further research in this area.

It was this study's expectation that initiating this small-scale study would bring understanding to or provide some insight about job satisfaction experiences of the forensic scientist personnel population. This researcher is very optimistic that this information will make law enforcement personnel more cognizant of factors that may cause their forensic scientists to become dissatisfied. Law enforcement personnel can then use this information as a framework to alleviate potential job dissatisfaction. It was predicted that this study would have limitations that may be helpful in guiding future research in the area of forensic scientist job satisfaction. It was further predicted that the shortcomings of this study would stimulate interest into the investigation of forensic scientist stress, attitudes, behaviors, and other similar areas.

SUMMARY

Review of the literature for Chapter Two has demonstrated that there is indeed a need for research in the area of job satisfaction and forensic scientists. There is a plethora of literature as it relates to police job satisfaction, correctional officer job satisfaction, and other types of law enforcement job satisfaction (Dowler, 2005). It is known that police, corrections, and other law enforcement personnel experience varying levels of stress and job satisfaction as a result of the nature of the job. However, when it comes to the amount of literature available on forensic scientist job satisfaction, this researcher found that research in this area is minimal. As demonstrated by Sewell (2000), extensive research has been done by researchers in nearly every area and subset of the law enforcement profession. To date there have been articles and various discussions on the *CSI* Effect. However, very little substantiative research has been done on how such variables as outsider's perception of forensic science work, duties of forensic science work et cetera affect forensic scientists and other forensic personnel. This lack of available research on forensic scientists and other forensic personnel demonstrates that this is an area very much in need of research. Research in this area is needed in order to find ways to better understand and assist this suddenly popular area of law enforcement.

Just as there is vast research to support the idea that job stress has a major impact on an individual's life and life satisfaction, the same can be said for job satisfaction. As stated by Rodes (2005), there is more than 30 years of research that have lead researchers to conclude that when one is satisfied with his job, that positive attitudinal satisfaction carries over into every aspect of that individual's life thus leading to life satisfaction. Job stress and job satisfaction or lack thereof exists in various areas of law enforcement such as corrections, police, probation, and law enforcement support personnel and there is an abundance of research to support such claims (Dowler, 2005). However, there appears to be no current peer reviewed research on whether or to what extent do forensic scientist experience job satisfaction. It should be noted that peer reviewed literature was also little to non-existent with regard to the kinds and amounts of stress experienced by forensic scientists. The researcher's expectation is that this study not only stimulates further research interests in forensic scientists and job satisfaction but also stimulate research of all forensic personnel in many other job related areas.

CHAPTER THREE
METHODOLOGY

INTRODUCTION

The purpose of this study was to examine how forensic scientists experience the role of job satisfaction in their daily employment setting. This chapter discusses the methodological components necessary to complete this study. Components such as researcher's philosophy, theoretical framework, research design, sampling design, measures, field testing, data collection, data analysis, and limitations to the study is discussed within this chapter.

RESEARCHER'S PHILOSOPHY

A qualitative research approach and the Moustakas (1994) phenomenological design is the theoretical framework guiding this study. The primary goal of this research was to understand and describe phenomena from the Participant's point of view (Creswell, 2003; Leedy & Ormrod, 2005; Mertens, 2005). For this basic qualitative study, phenomenological methods were used to collect and analyze data as well as interpret the findings. The descriptive phenomenology method was the ideal approach to take for this study because this approach allowed the researcher to gather Participants' perceptions or meaning of a specific experience or phenomena (Mertens, 2005). Additionally, this methodology allowed the researcher's to learn how individuals function in their daily lives and get to better understand the lived experiences of individuals being studied (Creswell, 2003; Neuman, 2003). In other words, this qualitative approach allowed the researcher's to gain a better understanding of how forensic scientists in a regional crime laboratory function on a daily basis. Most importantly, this approach allowed the researcher's to gather perspectives as to how these daily duties contribute to job satisfaction or dissatisfaction.

THEORETICAL FRAMEWORK

Frank Landy (1978) used Solomon and Corbit's (1973) opponent process theory philosophy to create his opponent process theory of job satisfaction. Solomon and Corbit's opponent process theory has been applied successfully in many different research areas. This successful application of the theory in other areas made it possible for opponent process theory to be generalized to an area such as job satisfaction (Bowling et al., 2005). Landy's opponent process theory appears to be the best fit to observe if job satisfaction changes over time even though the core duties of the job have not. This research was inquisitive as to exactly what are some of those workplace experiences that may influence job satisfaction among forensic scientists.

Using Landy's opponent process theory as theoretical support, this research sought to examine job satisfaction of forensic scientists. The desired result was data that would support the hypothesis that the job of forensic scientist is not necessarily higher or more significant as often depicted or perceived. Data for this study was gathered by interviewing individuals who are known within the field as forensic scientists.

RESEARCH DESIGN

The study employed a basic qualitative research design. Phenomenology was the type of qualitative research used to explore the experiences of forensic scientists with regard to job satisfaction. Phenomenological research allowed the researcher to study a small number of individuals in order to discover the essence of experiences regarding a particular phenomenon as described by the individuals being studied (Creswell, 2003). Moreover, phenomenology allowed Participants to reflect and respond in a more personal manner while sharing what they are experiencing and how the experiences are affecting them. This appeared to be the most appropriate method to examine forensic scientists and job satisfaction.

Qualitative data was collected to get an understanding of forensic scientist job satisfaction experiences. One-on-one interviews were appropriate for this study because it allowed the researcher's to use open-ended questions to invoke views and opinions from Participants (Creswell, 2003). This study employed the one-on-one interview technique with forensic scientists from each of the following category:

- Those employed as a forensic scientist 1-10 years.
- Those employed as a forensic scientist 11-21+ years.

The researcher's offered the Participants the option of conducting the interviews off site in a community type setting (library, Participant's home, et cetera). It was anticipated that an off site setting would allow the Participants to be more relaxed and allow them to speak more freely. If the forensic scientist requested that the interview be done at the job site in his office to better accommodate him, the researcher accommodated.

Audio taping was utilized in order to ensure that every aspect of the interview was captured. The use of audio taping was very helpful during the transcription and data analysis portion of the study, as it allowed for the recall of information more accurately.

SAMPLE DESIGN

Qualitative data was collected using purposive sampling to better understand job satisfaction experiences of forensic scientists. Sproull (2002) defines purposive sampling as a nonrandom sampling technique that is indiscriminately done because the sample population contains characteristics that the researcher believes is important for the research area to be studied. A purposive sampling strategy using recruitment flyers was used for this study because the goal was to discuss job satisfaction among specific forensic scientists and not generalize results to all forensic scientists that exist throughout the world.

Although using purposive sampling for this study proved advantageous because of the chosen population size, a possible disadvantage was the potential for bias due to the inability to random sample all forensic scientists who work in the forensic science field no matter the size of the setting, locale, or other factors (Sproull, 2002). A potential bias of generalizing experiences of this small group of forensic scientists to all forensic scientists could quite possibly cause issues within such a study. However, as stated earlier, the goal of this study was to evaluate job satisfaction among a specific group of forensic scientists and results would not be used to generalize to other or all forensic scientists that exist. As such, no anticipation of bias was expected due to the use of purposive sampling (Mertens, 2005). This study employed the one-on-one interview technique. One-on-one interviews were appropriate for this study because it allowed the researcher to use open-ended questions to invoke views and opinions from Participants (Creswell, 2003).

In qualitative phenomenological research, a Participant size of approximately six is considered sufficient (Mertens, 2005). Leedy and Ormrod (2005) even go as far as state that a typical sample size for a phenomenological study may be as small as five and as large as twenty-five Participants who must have direct awareness of the phenomena being examined. Limiting the study's participate number to eight allowed for a better organized study, interviews, and data collection. More importantly adhering to a small sample size allowed for better accuracy in data analysis and interpretation. It was researcher's opinion that more than eight Participants would cause the data analysis and interpretation to become cumbersome and less organized due to an over-abundance of information collected. Such would potentially be detrimental to the success of the study.

During the interview process of the original Participants if there were differences in responses additional Participants in each category would have been interviewed. At any point during the interview process if it was deemed that no new information was being yielded, the researcher would end the study. According to Mertens (2005), data collection or analysis should be terminated if the additional data does not contribute any new information.

The target population from which data for this study derived was from individuals employed in a crime laboratory setting. These individuals were targeted because they are known to work for a crime laboratory. Specifically, only those potential Participants known to be employed in their crime laboratory as forensic scientists were invited to participate. The use of recruitment flyers was the method for obtaining Participants. Only individuals identified as forensic scientists by their organization were given a recruitment flyer. Out of the interested Participants, only eight individuals were selected by the researcher to participate in one-on-one interviews. The researcher's selection of the eight Participants was based on the potential to fit into the following categories:

- Those employed as a forensic scientist 1-10 years.
- Those employed as a forensic scientist 11-20+ years.

As each interested forensic scientist Participant came forth, each was placed in the above categories until each category had been filled with the study's required number of Participants (four per category).

For the purposes of this study, all forensic scientists were considered only those individuals who perform forensic analysis of evidence within various areas of the forensic sciences (firearms, forensic chemistry, trace evidence, DNA, serology). Depending on the agency, a forensic scientist may be referred to simply as forensic scientist or by names that are technical sounding like criminalist or by a name that directly relates to their job such as Questioned Document Examiner or Latent Print Examiner.

The Participants selected for this study are classified by their organization as criminalists or according to their specialty (e.g. Questioned Document Examiner, Firearms Examiner, and Latent Print Examiner). For the purposes of this study, the criminalists and those classified according to their specialties who participated in this study were generically referred to as forensic scientists. Forensic personnel within a crime laboratory such as support staff, evidence technicians, property controllers, laboratory technicians, and student assistants who do not perform forensic analysis of evidence were excluded from this study.

A group setting for this study would not have been advantageous or the best method for this study as forensic scientists are exceptionally busy, are constantly under time constraints, and have varying work schedules. When permission was granted to conduct research, the researcher solicited forensic scientist to fit each category explained earlier and scheduled individual interviews. Once the eight forensic scientist confirmed that they would participate in the study, the researcher's arranged for a time, date, and place to conduct each interview. Instructions and all details were explained to the Participants when initial contact was made prior to the interview and again on the interview date.

The interviews were conducted in a setting and at a time that was conducive to the forensic scientists. Conducting the interviews in a setting and at a time that was favorable to the forensic scientists allowed the forensic scientists to be open in their responses. It was anticipated that some Participants would request to be interviewed in their offices on their own time (before work hours, lunch break, or after work hours) while other forensic scientists would feel more relaxed and free to answer questions regarding job satisfaction offsite. All Participants had no problems being interviewed in their offices on their own time.

A brief written explanation of the study and other pertinent information was organized prior to approaching the Participants. Each Participant who agreed to participate in the study was given the Informed Consent Form and other pertinent information. Participants were also given the opportunity to ask further questions regarding the study, privacy, and other concerns. Those individuals who wished to participate in the interview but who do not want to sign the Informed Consent Form were not allowed to participate.

Participants were advised that they may withdraw from the study at any time during the interview process. Participants were advised of this right prior to being given the Informed Consent Form, after signing the Informed Consent Form, and before commencement of the interview questions. The interviews were audio taped and transcribed at the conclusion of each individual interview. Participants were also ensured that all data associated with the study (audio tapes, transcriptions, emails, forms connected to the study) would be stored confidentially in the researcher's home office in a locked file according to suggested Institutional Review Board standards. The data will be stored for at least seven years from publication. The researcher's will be the only ones with access to the data stored in the locked file. When the researcher's deem that the stored information is no longer needed (seven years past publication), the data shall be destroyed in a manner that ensures all confidential information is unidentifiable using shredding methods.

MEASURES

A two-part Forensic Scientist Experiences Interview Guide developed by the researcher's was used to collect data from Participants. The interview guide for this semi-structured interview consists of open-ended questions that serve to elicit responses. The first part of the Forensic Scientist Experiences Interview Guide consists of demographic questions such as age, gender, and educational level. The second part of the guide consists of questions related to experiences forensic scientists may encounter in their daily employment setting that could play a role in job satisfaction. The Forensic Scientist Experiences Interview Guide answered the researcher's questions as well as allowed for Participants to give unsolicited information. This information also surprisingly proved useful in developing themes that were not initially anticipated by the researcher. The primary measures used in this qualitative study involved personal interviews using open-ended questions. The questions used were as follows:

DEMOGRAPHIC INFORMATION

1. What is your gender?
2. What is your age?
3. What is your current title at the crime laboratory?
4. What is/are your area(s) of expertise?
5. How long have you been employed at your current location?
6. How long have you been employed within the forensic science field?
7. What is your highest level of education?
8. Do you think that your current salary is commensurate to your education and the amount of work you do?

EXPERIENCES

1. What are some of the responsibilities required of your current position? How does this affect your overall views of the job?
2. How accurate do you think the media (fictitious and mainstream) portrays what a forensic scientist does to get the job done? How does this portrayal affect your daily job?
3. What are your thoughts with regard to fictitious forensic shows as to whether they help or hinder forensic science and the criminal justice process? How does it affect your daily job?
4. Compared to when you first started working as a forensic scientist would you say that you are as satisfied today as you were then?
5. How have things changed both technologically and professionally in forensic science since you started in the field and how have these changes affected your job satisfaction outlook?
6. What are some of the things that contribute to your job satisfaction (e.g. pay, peers, management, and burnout)?
7. How do you feel about newcomers to the field? Do you feel they have unreasonable expectations about forensic science because of "TV forensics"? Does this make your job more difficult?
8. Has your work in forensics enhanced your life and the lives of others? Has this contributed to your job satisfaction?
9. What do you feel can be done to promote forensic scientist job satisfaction, if any?

FIELD TESTING

Three experts in the field tested the Forensic Scientist Experiences Forensic Scientist Experiences Interview Guide. The experts consisted of a Quality Assurance Manager, Quality Assurance Officer, and an Assistant Laboratory

Director each of whom worked as a forensic scientist for well over 20 years each before holding their current crime laboratory upper management positions.

The field test involved having the three experts read the questions to determine the appropriateness for the study's goal. The experts' invaluable recommended changes included question structural changes, question deletions, and provision of questions that should be considered for the study.

All recommended changes where completed and the Forensic Scientist Experiences Interview Guide resubmitted to the experts for review. The experts reviewed and validated the Forensic Scientist Experiences Interview Guide as being reliable to elicit the necessary information to answer the study's research question.

DATA COLLECTION PROCEDURES

According to Creswell (2003), one reason a researcher may chose to use interviews to collect data is the fact that interviews allow Participants to bring forth their views and opinions about the subject at hand. Data for this qualitative study was collected using one-on-one interviews with eight forensic scientists. A group setting for this study was not advantageous or the best method for this study as forensic scientists are exceptionally busy, are constantly under time constraints, and have varying work schedules. Once permission from the university, Institutional Review Board, and the selected forensic scientists had been obtained by the researcher, the interviewing commenced. The interviews were audio taped and transcribed once the interviews were completed.

For this qualitative research study, the data collection technique used was methods and procedures recommended by Moustakas (1994) for collecting phenomenological data. All data from the one-on-one interviews was collected by adhering to the following steps:

1. The researcher's role in the investigation process was judgment free when it came to the phenomena being investigated. In the transcendental phenomenological approach this is known as the Epoche process.
2. The researcher developed a set of questions or topics to guide the interview process.
3. The researcher conducted and recorded a lengthy one-on-one interview that focused on a bracketed topic and question.
4. If necessary, the researcher conducted follow-up interviews (Moustakas, 1994).

Upon making successful contact, the researcher arranged for a time, date, and place to conduct each interview. Instructions and all details were explained to the Participants when initial contact was made, prior to the interview, and again when the Participants arrived for the interview. Each Participant who agreed to participate in the study was given the Informed Consent Form and other pertinent information. Participants were advised that they may withdraw from the study at any time. Those individuals who wished to participate in the interview but who did not want to sign the Informed Consent Form were not allowed to participate. Participants were also given the opportunity to ask further questions regarding the study, privacy, and other concerns.

The researcher conducted audio taped individual semi-structured interview sessions asking each forensic scientist open-ended questions from the prepared Forensic Scientist Experiences Interview Guide. It was anticipated the interviews would last no longer than an hour in length. A tape recorder was used to aid in transcription once the interviews were completed. The primary reason for audio taping the interviews was to ensure that credibility issues did not arise during transcription because pertinent information was lost or misinterpreted by the researcher. To ensure individual anonymity, the Participants were protected by using a non-identifier such as Participant 1, Participant 2 and so forth on the Forensic Scientist Experiences Interview Guide. To ensure confidentiality, as each interview was completed the researcher stored the data in a secure location.

All data collected was stored confidentially in the researcher's home office in a locked file according to recommended Institutional Review Board standards. The researcher is the only one with access to the data stored in the locked file. The data will be stored for at least seven years from publication. When the researcher's deem that the stored information is no longer needed, the data shall be destroyed in a manner that ensures all confidential information is unidentifiable.

DATA ANALYSIS PROCEDURES

In qualitative research, data analysis involves making sense of the text and image data that has been collected (Creswell, 2003). Equally, in qualitative research data analysis' main goal is to identify recurring themes from descriptions of individual's experiences and present the results as viewed through the eyes of the individual's who experienced the phenomena (Leedy & Ormrod, 2005). The current study took the completed audio taped interviews and transcribed verbatim producing potentially viable raw data.

In order to distinguish whether the quality of the raw data collected for the intended study was viable; an effective data analysis procedure must be in place. For this qualitative research study, the data analysis technique followed was a modified version of the Moustakas (1994) van Kaam's method of phenomenological data analysis. The six steps used in this method for phenomenological data analysis for this study included:

1. Listing and preliminary grouping every expression that was relevant to the experience.
2. Reducing and eliminating any irrelevant text. For example, text that was repetitive, had nothing to do with the topic or questions asked was reduced or eliminated.
3. Clustering the constant elements of the experiences into a theme.
4. Validating the constant elements and their themes by checking them against the Participants' transcribed interviews.

5. Using the validated constant elements and themes, constructing an Individual Textural Description for each Participant's lived experience.
6. Incorporating the constant elements and themes, constructing for each Participant a Textural-Structural Description of the meanings and essences of the experience (Moustakas, 1994).

The modified version of Moustakas' van Kaam method for data analysis allowed the researcher to transcribe and analyze the raw data into useful information with regard to the job satisfaction experiences among selected forensic scientists. This raw data was used to extract any emerging themes from the interviews.

LIMITATIONS OF METHODOLOGY AND STRATEGIES FOR MINIMIZING IMPACT

A limitation of using a phenomenological design methodology for this study was that it could potentially have an influence on the results of the study and how the results were interpreted by the researcher's. The researcher's remained unbiased and ensured that all preconceived ideologies on forensic science and job satisfaction experiences did not enter the data collection and interpretation process. The validity of the study was upheld by keeping the focus on the forensic scientists' reported lived job satisfaction experiences and not any preconceived researcher opinions.

CREDIBILITY

According to Trochim (2006), credibility involves making sure that the results of qualitative research are credible or believable from the perspective of those participating in the research. In qualitative research, the role of reliability is relatively minor whereas validity is viewed as having a significant role when it comes to qualitative inquiries (Creswell, 2003). Though validity or truth is significant, qualitative researchers tend to focus not necessarily on validity but more on authenticity (Neuman, 2003). To ensure that the authenticity of the data was credible and accurate, member checking was used. As said by Mertens (2005), member checks are the most significant factor when trying to ascertain credibility. Member checking involves taking the transcribed information from the interviews back to the Participants and have each Participant verify that the transcription accurately represents the statements given (Creswell, 2003; Mertens, 2005). Once each Participant reviewed the transcript of the interview and verified that everything was correct, each Participant was provided the opportunity to add further comments. If further comments were provided, the researcher's would have transcribed and again member checked. No further comments were provided.

Since this was an instrument developed by the researcher's, the Forensic Scientist Experiences Interview Guide was distributed to three experts in the field of forensic science for review. The Forensic Scientist Experiences Interview Guide was reviewed and validated by the three experts as being a reliable instrument that would effectively gather data to support the research question. These experts in the field were once forensic scientists who performed casework daily but are now employed in administrative capacities in a major forensic crime laboratory system. The reviewers were a Quality Assurance Manager; a Quality Assurance Officer; and an Assistant Laboratory Director. Each reviewer has been employed within the forensic science field and working within the forensic laboratory setting for well over twenty years.

TRANSFERABILITY

Transferability in qualitative research refers to the extent to which the results of the study can be generalized to other contexts or settings (Trochim, 2006). The transferability of results from this qualitative study may be limited due to a small sample size and the fact that all the forensic scientists happen to be employed by the same crime laboratory. As such, the study is not generalizable to all forensic scientists that exist in the world and at other locations.

EXPECTED FINDINGS

It was anticipated that forensic scientists participating in this study experienced more job dissatisfaction than the public and organizations employing forensic scientists realize. It was further anticipated that much of the job dissatisfaction the forensic scientists report would be due to such factors as organizational demands, caseload, time constraints, and inadequate salary. Based on such anticipated results, it was inferred that real-life forensic work was not as easy, exaggeratedly satisfying or as glamorous as the media propaganda depicts.

ETHICAL ISSUES

According to Sproull (2002), the purpose of having in place ethical research practices is to protect Participants in research studies and protect Participants' rights and keep them from being psychologically or physically harmed. When it comes to ethical issues in research there are four areas where problems could occur: privacy rights, protection from harm, informed consent, and honesty in reporting findings. Simply stated when conducting research:
1. The Participants' right to privacy should be respected
2. Participants should be protected from harm
3. Participants must be informed of the nature of the study so as to make an informed decision of whether or not to participate and;
4. Lastly, the researcher should be completely honest when reporting the outcome of the research even if the findings do not support the hypothesis (Leedy & Ormrod, 2005).

Prior to commencement of the study, the Participants for this study were given detailed explanations of the study to be read prior to the interviews. Administration of the study's purpose prior to interviewing was done so that the Participants can make an informed decision to determine whether they wished to participate in the study (Sproull, 2002). All guidelines with regard to ethical treatment of humans set by the Institutional Review Board were strictly adhered to in order to maintain ethical standards pertaining to the treatment of human Participants.

CONCLUSION

This phenomenology study explored how forensic scientists experience the role of job satisfaction in their daily employment setting. Research in the area of forensic science as well as forensic scientist job satisfaction is rather limited. It was the goal of this study to provide insightful information with respect to job satisfaction experiences of forensic scientists to stimulate future interest in the study of forensic scientists. The research question for this study was how do forensic scientists' daily employment setting experiences play a role in job satisfaction? The research question at hand was explored using Landy's opponent process theory as theoretical support. A qualitative research approach and the Moustakas (1994) phenomenological design was used to analyze the data. The data was collected by conducting one-on-one interviews with eight forensic scientists using open-ended questions. It was optimistic that the data collected from this study would give forensic organizations an insight into the experiences of forensic personnel. Additionally, it was this study's wish that the data collected and interpreted from this study would stimulate further research interests of the thoughts, attitudes, and behaviors of forensic scientists.

CHAPTER FOUR
DATA COLLECTION AND ANALYSIS

INTRODUCTION

The function of this chapter is to provide the results of data collection, data analysis, and to share some of the phenomenological experiences of forensic scientists. The purpose of this phenomenological based study was to explore job satisfaction experiences among a select group of forensic scientists. The descriptive phenomenology method was the ideal approach to take for this study because this approach allowed the researcher to gather Participants' perceptions or meaning of a specific experience or phenomena (Mertens, 2005). The study used a modified version of the Moustakas van Kaam method to analyze the transcribed audio taped interviews to assist with finding relevant themes located in the data.

Eight forensic scientists, four females and four males, were asked to describe their job satisfaction experiences working as a forensic scientist. For the purposes of this study, only those individuals who perform forensic analysis of evidence within various areas of the forensic sciences (firearms, forensic chemistry, trace evidence, DNA, serology) were solicited to participate. Depending on the agency, a forensic scientist may be referred to simply as forensic scientist or by names that are technical sounding like criminalist or by a name that directly relates to their job such as Questioned Document Examiner or Latent Print Examiner. The Participants selected for this study are classified by their organization as criminalists or according to their specialty (e.g. Questioned Document Examiner, Firearms Examiner, and Latent Print Examiner). For the purposes of this study, the criminalists and those classified according to their specialties who participated in this study were generically referred to as forensic scientists.

The research question was how do forensic scientists' daily employment setting experiences play a role in job satisfaction? The study's focus was to explore job satisfaction experiences of forensic scientists. The researcher's used audio taped individual semi-structured interview sessions to ask each forensic scientist open-ended questions from the prepared Forensic Scientist Experiences Interview Guide as it relates to job satisfaction.

The researcher's solicited Participants by making direct contact with known forensic scientists. The study sought eight volunteers to participate. As volunteers were solicited and agreed to participate in the study the researcher immediately categorized volunteers into the following categories:
- Those employed as a forensic scientist 1-10 years.
- Those employed as a forensic scientist 11-21+ years.

The solicited individuals were approached based on their potential to fit into the aforementioned categories. The researcher's continued solicitation of volunteers until each category was filled with four Participants. The recruitment process took about a week. Once the number of required Participants was acquired the researcher followed up with the Participants a week later and scheduled a time to conduct individual interviews. The interviews were scheduled for a day and time that was convenient for each individual Participant.

THE RESEARCHER

The phenomenon under study, forensic scientist job satisfaction, has been of interest to the researcher's for quite some time. Indeed the field of forensic science is a fascinating one and so are the majority of the individuals who work in the field. The field began to garner an exceptionally large amount of attention when the popularity of such shows as *CSI: Las Vegas* emerged. As a result of such notoriety, the image of being a forensic scientist has gone from being just a boring laboratory worker to one of being hip and ubercool. With this sudden awareness of forensic science also came an equally sudden overwhelming workload.

Working in Questioned Documents can be hectic as well as frustrating. Constantly being bombarded by requests for services that don't exist or requests that are beyond the department's capabilities (such as having an analysis completed within 24 hours) because someone saw it on *CSI* or other forensic show can grow tiresome after a while. The researcher's wanted to know just how satisfied forensic scientists were in their daily work environment. Additionally, the researcher's hoped to discover whether factors such as misperceptions of forensic scientists and their capabilities play a role in that satisfaction (e.g. being compared to TV forensic scientists).

PARTICIPANTS' DEMOGRAPHIC CHARACTERISTICS

Certain demographic profile characteristics where gathered from the Participants. Information with reference to gender, age, job title, area of expertise, years employed at current locale, years employed within the forensic science field, education level, and salary information was gathered from each Participant. The Participant responses to these questions can be viewed in Table 4.1.

Table 4.1: Participant (P) Demographics

	Gender	Age	Job Title	Area of Expertise	Yrs at Location	Yrs in Field	Degree	Satisfied w/ Salary
P1	F	37	Sr. Criminalist	Controlled Substances	12	12	BS Criminalistics	Yes
P2	F	35	Criminalist	Biology DNA Crime Scene	5	6	BS Biochemistry	Yes
P3	M	54	Sr. Criminalist	DNA Crime Scene Biology Trace Evidence Narcotics Blood Alcohol Breath Alcohol	1.5	32.5	MS Biology	Yes
P4	F	35	Criminalist	Controlled Substances	3	5	BS Biology	Yes & No
P5	M	51	Sr. Criminalist	DNA Biology Crime Scene	15	21	BS Chemistry	Yes
P6	M	25	Criminalist	Blood Alcohol Breath Alcohol	2	2	BS Biology	Yes
P7	M	47	Sr. Criminalist	Firearms Biology	11	11.5	MS Criminalistics	Yes
P8	F	26	Criminalist	Biology	2	2	MS Criminalistics	Yes

To maintain anonymity, Participants were not referred to by name during the research process. Each Participant was referred to as Participant 1, Participant 2, Participant 3, and so on. Eight Participants were chosen by the researcher first and foremost because they were eligible for the categories that the study sought:
- Those employed as a forensic scientist 1-10 years.
- Those employed as a forensic scientist 11-21+ years.

The sample size, eight Participants, consisted of four female forensic scientists and four male forensic scientists. The age range of the Participants was 25 to 54 years old. The Participants had experience working in the field of forensic science that ranged from to years to over thirty-two years. Though the forensic discipline of each Participant varied, all Participants had college degrees in chemistry, biology, or criminalistics. The Participants had varying law enforcement agency experiences ranging from having never worked in a law enforcement agency setting prior to current employer to having worked for one or more other law enforcement agencies prior to current employer.

INTERVIEW GUIDE QUESTIONS

This study wanted to explore job satisfaction experiences of forensic scientists and asked the following question: *How do forensic scientists' daily employment setting experiences play a role in job satisfaction?* The Forensic Scientist Experiences Interview Guide was used to gather information from the forensic scientists. The Guide consisted of seventeen structured questions related to aspects of the forensic scientists' work experiences. The first eight questions were demographic questions that asked the following:
1. What is your gender?
2. What is your age?
3. What is your current title at the crime laboratory?
4. What is/are your area(s) of expertise?
5. How long have you been employed at your current location?
6. How long have you been employed within the forensic science field?
7. What is your highest level of education?
8. Do you think that your current salary is commensurate to your education and the amount of work you do?

The second set of questions in the Forensic Scientist Interview Guide included questions that were related to the Participants' job experiences. The questions were as follows:
1. What are some of the responsibilities required of your current position? How does this affect your overall views of the job?
2. How accurate do you think the media (fictitious and mainstream) portrays what a forensic scientist does to get the job done? How does this portrayal affect your daily job?

3. What are your thoughts with regard to fictitious forensic shows as to whether they help or hinder forensic science and the criminal justice process? How does it affect your daily job?
4. Compared to when you first started working as a forensic scientist would you say that you are as satisfied today as you were then?
5. How have things changed both technologically and professionally in forensic science since you started in the field and how have these changes affected your job satisfaction outlook?
6. What are some of the things that contribute to your job satisfaction (e.g. pay, peers, management, and burnout)?
7. How do you feel about newcomers to the field? Do you feel they have unreasonable expectations about forensic science because of "TV forensics"? Does this make your job more difficult?
8. Has your work in forensics enhanced your life and the lives of others? Has this contributed to your job satisfaction?
9. What do you feel can be done to promote forensic scientist job satisfaction, if any?

The interview questions were analyzed for themes, descriptions, and meaning units (Creswell, 2003; Moustakas, 1994).

PARTICIPANT PROFILES

This study had eight Participants and the following is a profile synopsis of each Participant. Names were not utilized in this study in order to protect the Participants' privacy and to make certain confidentiality was maintained. In a one-on-one interview format, each Participant discussed his or her job satisfaction experiences working as a forensic scientist.

PARTICIPANT 1

Participant 1 was a 37-year old female whose official title is Senior Criminalist. She is a forensic analyst assigned to the controlled substances (drugs) section of the forensic laboratory. The Participant stated that her primary duties daily are to "examine suspected controlled substances evidence from various law enforcement agencies". She is also involved with the quality assurance program for the Bureau. Participant 1 has been employed with this particular forensic laboratory and the field of forensic science for twelve years.

PARTICIPANT 2

Participant 2 was a 35-year old female whose official title is Criminalist. The Participant is assigned to the biology section of the laboratory and currently training in DNA and crime scenes. The Participant stated that she is responsible for analyzing evidence for bodily fluids such as semen, saliva, and blood. According to the Participant, this analysis process also includes "documenting the evidence and maintaining a proper chain of custody, writing reports to discuss findings, and testifying in court". Participant 2 has been employed with her current forensic laboratory for five years and prior to that, she worked at another forensic laboratory (within the same system) for two years.

PARTICIPANT 3

Participant 3 was a 54-year old male whose official title is Senior Criminalist. The Participant also conveyed that he is also considered Technical Lead for the DNA section. The Participant states that "DNA Technical Leaders in laboratories are responsible for the oversight of training, quality assurance, method development, and general quality assurance in the DNA laboratory." Participant 3's area of expertise include DNA, crime scenes, blood spatter reconstruction, breath alcohol, narcotics, and some trace evidence. The Participant has worked for several forensic laboratories in the past and has over 32 years of experience in the field of forensic science. He has been at the current forensic laboratory for almost two years.

PARTICIPANT 4

Participant 4 was 35-year old female and she is employed as a Criminalist within the controlled substances (drugs) section in the forensic laboratory. According to Participant 4, her job is to "examine evidence that comes in that is suspected controlled substances and write a report on the findings which typically involves going to court to testify to those findings". She has been employed with the field of forensics for about five years and employed at the current location for a little over three years.

PARTICIPANT 5

Participant 5 was a 51-year old male who is employed as a Senior Criminalist within the forensic laboratory. He currently works in the DNA/forensic biology program. According to the Participant, his job entails performing casework and DNA analysis which includes "assessing the details of the case and determine what questions are trying to be answered which may not always be obvious". In addition, the Participant stated that he also works crime scenes and that he has worked in other areas of forensic science. Participant 5 has been employed at the current forensic laboratory for about fifteen years but has worked within the forensic science field for well over twenty-one years.

PARTICIPANT 6

Participant 6 was a 25-year old male who is employed as a Criminalist within the forensic laboratory. The Participant is currently assigned to the breath and alcohol laboratory. The breath and alcohol section analyzes breath, blood, and urine samples taken from drivers involved in DUI (driving under the influence) investigations. According to the Participant, breath, blood, and urine samples are analyzed for the presence or absence of alcohol. The Participant is also responsible for training law enforcement personnel on the use of breath instruments (typically used in the field by police officers). Participant 6 has been employed within the field of forensic science and at the current forensic laboratory for about two years.

PARTICIPANT 7

Participant 7 was a 47-year old male employed as a Senior Criminalist within the forensic laboratory. His areas of expertise are firearms examination and biology screening. Currently Participant 7 works within the firearms section. According to the Participant, "firearms examination is primarily attempting to determine whether or not a specific cartridge case or bullet was fired from a specific weapon or whether multiple cartridge cases or bullets were fired from the same gun and then determine if they were fired from a specific weapon and then other ancillary examinations that go along with it like distance determination". Participant 7 has been employed within the forensic science field for almost twelve years. He has been employed at the current forensic laboratory for eleven years.

PARTICIPANT 8

Participant 8 was a 26-year old female employed as a Criminalist in the forensic laboratory. She is currently assigned to the biology section where she conducts biology screening for blood, semen, saliva, and urine on evidence. Participant 8 has been employed at the current forensic laboratory and within the field of forensic science for approximately two years.

DATA COLLECTION

The data collection process for this study included conducting interviews, transcription of the interviews, and then analyzing the job satisfaction experiences of the eight forensic scientists. Analysis of the data produced an assortment of themes that were the result of the job satisfaction experiences of the forensic scientists. The themes and possible meanings were extracted utilizing a modified version of the van Kaam method devised by Moustakas (1994).

Over the course of about one week, eight forensic scientists were interviewed by the researcher's. Each Participant was asked 17 questions (eight demographic and nine related to experiences) during a one-on-one interview with the researcher. Each interview lasted between 25 to 45 minutes. The length of each interview was determined by the responses given by the Participant. All the interviews were audio taped and then transcribed by the researcher's. When approached for the study, the Participants were very eager to participate. The Participants were elated that someone was actually interested in their lived on the job experiences. Some Participants explained that it was about time that the voice of forensic scientists be heard regarding the true nature of the field to dispel many of the fallacies that exist about forensic scientists due to the *CSI* Effect.

The Participants' eagerness to assist this study by sharing their job satisfaction experiences was somewhat unanticipated. The researcher had some fears that the study would be somewhat limited because Participants would not be completely forthcoming with their responses for fear of their management finding out their thoughts about the job. These fears were quickly dispelled once the interview process began and substantive information was being contributed. The Participants all stated that the field is lacking in research with regard to the needs and issues that forensic scientists must face on a regular basis and that they were delighted to participate in the study. Some Participants expressed that it was about time that researchers began taking a closer look at some of the issues forensic scientists experience.

Each of the eight interviews began with the researcher reiterating the nature of the study and what was expected of the Participant. Following the explanation, the informed consent and confidentiality forms were presented for signatures and the Participant was asked if he still agreed to continue with the study. At each interview session (eight total), the Participant agreed to continue with the study. Once the researcher's received the signed forms, the Participants were asked if they had any other questions or concerns. Once those questions or concerns were addressed, the interviews commenced.

The rationale for the interview questions was to explore the lived experiences of forensic scientists to answer the following question: How do forensic scientists' daily employment setting experiences play a role in job satisfaction? The questions derived from the Forensic Scientist Experiences Interview Guide developed by the researcher. All responses were audio taped to ensure accuracy in data recall. Transcripts were produced from the audio tapes after the interviews were completed. The transcript from each interview was analyzed using a modified version of the Moustakas van Kaam method.

When conducting research, researchers are often encouraged to use a process known as epoche. Epoche (Moustakas 1994) is the process where the researcher makes a conscious effort to put aside any prejudices or prejudgments regarding the phenomena being investigated to ensure that the study will be free of biases or other preconceived ideas based on prior knowledge or experiences. Epoche also requires that the researcher be not only open and receptive but to also listen without judgment of the Participants' experiences so as to gain a clear understanding of the phenomena being observed or studied (Moustakas, 1994). No bias or prejudgments were made by the researcher during the research process.

DATA ANALYSIS

The data analysis technique followed was a modified version of the Moustakas (1994) van Kaam method of phenomenological data analysis. The modified version of the Moustakas van Kaam method required:
1. *Listing and preliminary grouping (horizonalization)*: Every expression that was relevant to the job satisfaction experience of forensic scientists was grouped.
2. *Reduction and elimination of any irrelevant text*: Any information given by the Participant that was repetitive and/or did not have any relevance to the topic of forensic scientist job satisfaction experiences was eliminated.
3. *Cluster the constant elements of the experience into a theme*: Themes were developed from clustered information.
4. *Validate the constant elements and their themes by checking them against the Participants' transcribed interviews*: Any clusters or themes that were observed were compared to the Participants' transcribed interviews to ensure accuracy.
5. *Using the validated constant elements and themes, construct an Individual Textural Description for each Participant's lived experience*: Using themes, each individual's transcribed interviews were used to extract verbatim accounts of each lived experience.
6. *Incorporating the constant elements and themes, construct for each Participant a Textural-Structural Description of the meanings and essences of the experience* (Moustakas, 1994): Using themes a description of meanings and essences of the experiences were constructed for each Participant.

A modified version of the Moustakas van Kaam method for data analysis allowed the researcher's to transcribe and analyze the raw data into useful information with regard to the job satisfaction experiences among selected forensic scientists. This raw data was used to extract any emerging themes from the interviews.

DATA CLUSTERING AND THEMATIZING

Moustakas (1994) states that data clustering and thematizing involves grouping any data uncovered by the Participant into core themes. By clustering the invariant constituents, the core themes of the experiences are revealed (Moustakas, 1994). With the assistance of the Moustakas phenomenological analysis method, textural-structural descriptions of the Participants' interviews were developed. Data clustering and thematizing along with the study's nine interview questions related to experiences provided empirical support for the themes indentified in the study.

RESEARCH FINDINGS

Upon preliminary analysis of the Participants' transcripts, recurring words and phrases emerged that allowed the researcher to categorize meaning units. These meaning units were an account of the researcher's understanding of the importance of the forensic scientist job satisfaction phenomena. The following key meaning units were observed:
- Fictitious portrayal of the job of forensic scientist
- Expect to get results quickly like on TV
- Forensic shows hinders process somewhat (*CSI* Effect)
- Satisfied with job
- Feeling of satisfaction from helping victim/community/society

Further analysis of the forensic scientist's interview transcripts was conducted using a modified version of the Moustakas (1994) van Kaam method. The transcripts' meaning units were analyzed more in-depth for emerging themes. Based on the textual data, specifically the meaning units extracted from that data from the forensic scientists' interviews, five central themes emerged:
- Comparison to forensics on TV
- Unrealistic expectations from others
- *CSI* Effect hinders job
- Job is satisfying
- Work affects lives of others

THEME ONE: COMPARISON TO FORENSICS ON TV

FICTITIOUS PORTRAYAL OF THE JOB OF FORENSIC SCIENTISTS

Perhaps one of the leading irritants to several Participants was that they as forensic scientists are constantly being compared to TV forensics or to the forensic scientist characters on TV. One Participant was quite blunt and said that he generally does not watch forensic shows because he knows that they are fictitious and they are incredibly irritating. The researcher's learned from the Participants that there are a lot of inaccuracies and misconceptions on TV. A few Participants think that these portrayals affect their jobs the most when it comes to the jury in court proceedings. It is up to a jury to determine guilt and innocence and if the jury has misperceptions on what forensic scientists and forensic science is capable of doing, then they can sometimes reach wrong decisions because the evidence results or the forensic scientist is not as they saw on TV. The typical juror expects the forensic scientist expert to do things that the forensic scientist simply is not capable of doing.
Continuing the interview on how the forensic scientists is portrayed on TV, one Participant revealed to the researcher:

Roles on TV where they're experts in every section or they go out to the scene and then they go back to the lab and do all the analysis is just not real. Many forensic scientists do not go to the field. I'm not involved in crime scenes, I'm only in the lab.

Other Participants concurred that even though the average individual, officers, and district attorney's know that they are watching TV, they still are under the assumption that the crime laboratory can do such things as turn a DNA case around in two hours or solve a crime for them in one day. Participant 4 became very animated when describing her encounters with individuals outside the forensic science field whose only understanding or the majority of their understanding of forensic science is via TV:

They'll say "well those people on *CSI* they will interview suspects and they carry guns, and they're out here and there and like they get their results like in minutes." Every once in a while you will get a new DA coming in saying "well how come you can't figure out what this is or you know talk about the timing."

As communicated by all the Participants, getting scientific results in minutes on evidence processed is simply not possible.

When talking about explaining real forensic scientists to the misinformed, Participants echoed that depending on their mood they may not tell people they work at a crime lab because once they do then the next statement is "oh, like *CSI*." Participants stated that after such a remark then they must start explaining the difference between *CSI* or shows like *CSI* and real forensics. One Participant just threw up his hands and said there are just some days that he simply is not in the mood for differentiating between the two because it can be exasperating. Therefore, he just tells people that he is employed in some other field that sounds less exciting or needs no explanation.

The overall lived experiences of the Participants on the issue of being compared to forensics on TV is one of extreme frustration because as one Participant divulged TV is for entertainment purposes but a lot of people forget or don't realize that and expect what they see on TV to be the same in real life. Thus, if an individual sees a particular process or technique on TV, with regard to forensics, they automatically think that such a process a) exists and that b) it works as simply and quickly as they saw it performed on television. Forensic science and being a forensic scientist just is not that effortless.

THEME TWO: UNREALISTIC EXPECTATIONS FROM OTHERS

EXPECT TO GET RESULTS QUICKLY LIKE ON TV

The second theme that emerged related to how Participants felt about what is expected from them as forensic scientists. Shows such as the *CSI* franchise, *NCIS*,

Bones and the like have become tremendously popular among this generation. Because of such media, the public has a predetermined idea of what a forensic scientist is and what the job of a forensic scientist necessitates. Responses given by the Participants showed that what incensed many of them was the fact that a majority of the people outside the field have a lot of erroneous information about forensic science and forensic scientists.

There is a major misconception that forensic analysis is completed at a rapid pace and that results are produced instantaneously, and that is simply not the case. Current media depiction also has the public believing that forensic science has exceptional scientific analytical capabilities as well. These were the areas that the Participants were quick to dispel myths. With regard to public perception, Participant 5 said:

> They have a misperception of the amount of work that we do. They think that we analyze every piece of evidence from the crime scene and we don't. We're only capable of looking at a small fraction and because we are only looking at the evidence that's the most pertinent to answering the questions that ends up being the small fraction of evidence and a lot of the other evidence isn't going to answer any questions so we don't analyze it. But they think we're supposed to analyze everything.

Several other Participants provided similar responses while sharing their frustrations that one of the hardest parts of their jobs is explaining to the public, sometimes even law enforcement personnel, that the technology that they saw on TV is non-existent or that it exists in limited form and results can not be swiftly produced.

The Participants affirmed that all these unrealistic expectations about what can be done and what types of analysis and outcomes you can actually obtain from doing certain procedures cause individuals to develop a false sense of expectations. One particular frustration with police officials involves the notion that DNA solves every crime. One Participant, Participant 8, specifically communicated to the researcher an example regarding touch DNA (only a very small sample or "touch" of DNA is needed for analysis). The Participant said that there is constant questioning from police officials asking "why can't you get my suspect's DNA from her vaginal swabs" because the police official heard via TV or other media about touch DNA. Because of that tidbit of information, the police official and others now have the perception that touch DNA is the most powerful forensic tool in the world when actually it is not.

Another annoyance expressed by the Participants when it comes to unrealistic expectations from forensically unaware individuals is the perceptions about how casework is conducted. The Participants revealed that the idea people have is that forensic scientists solve every case as they come in and do so in an expedient manner. As Participant 8 stated, some police officials bring in evidence and ask "can I have this by the next day". The Participants each gave varying explanations of how casework is typically completed within the crime laboratory. Mentioned repeatedly was how significantly backlogged the cases were, so no, cases are not solved as soon as they enter the laboratory. One Participant further explained:

> Many of them [cases] are going to court, many of them need to be worked and we just don't have the time to say "hey give me your case and I'll work it in an hour". That's ridiculous.

As interpreted by the researcher, the overall lived experiences of the Participants on the issue of expectations of forensic scientists by the public and surprisingly some law enforcement personnel is that many people outside the field do not truly comprehend the depth of the job of forensic scientist or the true capabilities of forensic science.

THEME THREE: *CSI* EFFECT HINDERS JOB

FORENSIC SHOWS HINDERS PROCESS SOMEWHAT (*CSI* EFFECT)

The third theme that emerged centers on the idea of whether or not all the forensic media in existence today give support to or hinders the forensic science community. Overwhelmingly, Participants agreed that it does both but Participants believe that there is more hindrance occurring because of what has been termed the *CSI* Effect. Briefly, the *CSI* Effect is a term coined to describe what happens when individuals, typically jurors, have expectations or make decisions because of what was viewed on shows such as *CSI*.

Many of the Participants were in agreement that the largest hindrance in the criminal justice process due to the *CSI* Effect is indeed in the area of the courts:

> Forensic shows hinders the process in terms of reaching correct conclusions or decisions in a jury trail because they [jurors] might think we do more than we're capable of. It's more of a challenge to explain to jurors or come up with answers to their questions basically because they're already programmed to thinking a certain way of what we do and what we are capable of [*CSI* Effect].

The Participant experiences further revealed, with regard to the courts and *CSI* Effect, that often jurors will deliberate not necessarily based on all the information received from witnesses, experts and so forth but on information viewed on television shows. A Participant expressed his disbelief that judges often feed into this *CSI* Effect as well:

> Sometimes judges will impart that vision [what jurors have seen on TV shows] in a jurors mind as to who a forensic analyst is and they'll [judges] say "oh it's similar to what you see on *CSI*" which is not the case.

Participants communicated that such incidences are not supposed to occur but unfortunately they do and it has been having a major impact on the court system and the judicial process as a whole. Further discussion of the perceived hindrances expressed by the Participants revolved around the fact that people who do not understand forensic science have high expectations. When these expectations fall short the individuals think that forensic science or the forensic scientists has failed when that is not the case. People are purely relying on false information, which in turn leads to, unbeknownst to them, false expectations.

The researcher's concluded from the particular lived experience that although there are hindrances experienced, *CSI* Effect, the Participants hesitantly appreciates forensic shows because the shows bring forensic science awareness. A major result of this awareness is that the field and agencies may get funding and even laws passed in favor of forensic science. Participants articulated that because of the forensic shows, more people have become not only more interested in the field of forensic science but there is also a renewed interest in science again. Participants point out that proof of an increase interest in forensic science can be seen by examining the number of colleges that now offer forensic programs. Some colleges have gone from offering certificates to offering actual four-year and even graduate degrees in forensic science. Something that was not possible just a few short years ago.

THEME FOUR: JOB IS SATISFYING

SATISFIED WITH JOB

The majority of the Participants stated that they were satisfied with their role of forensic scientist. The recurring theme amongst the Participants with regard to being a forensic scientist is that even though their caseloads or amount of work they do outweighs the amount they are paid, they are always under time constraints or must deal with negative attitudes from outside sources, they are satisfied with the job.

Participants expressed varying types of satisfaction. Things such as reaching senior status, being more involved in the process, and even being more involved in day-to-day activities were found to be satisfying to the Participants. One Participant stated that knowing that she is helping the criminal process along and not just doing job tasks that are meaningless is one of the things that adds to her job satisfaction. Participant 3 specifically said:

> I'm actually probably more satisfied now than I was then because I know a lot more. I think I'm to the point in my expertise where I know what I don't know. Which sounds strange but is a good place to be. I feel comfortable with what I've done and other things so I'm satisfied.

In general, Participants also acknowledged being more satisfied now than when they first entered the field because of such factors as the training they have received, the amount of responsibility they now have, opportunities to participate in peer related conferences, and so forth has made them feel more established as a forensic scientist. This is in total contrast to when they first started as a forensic scientist and their duties consisted of reading manuals, doing busy work, and other tasks that had more of an assembly line feel to them making them feel like they were still a student in college.

The overall lived experiences observed by the researcher is that the Participants are highly satisfied with their jobs and that if they had to chose a career all over again, they would still select forensic science and the job of being a forensic scientist. Admittedly, said one Participant, there are satisfying days and dissatisfying days as with any job but there are not so many dissatisfying days that it would make them not like being a forensic scientist.

THEME FIVE: WORK AFFECTS LIVES OF OTHERS

FEELING OF SATISFACTION FROM HELPING VICTIM/COMMUNITY/ SOCIETY

The final emergent theme involved the Participant's feelings about how their work affects the lives of others connected to the cases in which they analyze. The Participants discussed with the researcher how in addition to forensic scientist related duties they often have many duties that are beyond what are in their job descriptions. Many of these tasks are considered menial by some Participants. Having to deal with these menial tasks could potentially lead the forensic scientist to be slightly negative about the job experience. However, several Participants stated that such does not interfere with their job satisfaction because they know they are doing the work for a good cause: to help others.

The consensus among the Participants was that everything done in forensics somehow affects someone's life. The Participants further articulated that there are not too many jobs that one can do as a career where you have experiences affecting people's lives in such a major way on a day-to-day basis. Without forensic science, the outcomes or victories that the forensic scientist achieves in court for victims and people that are affected negatively by crime would not be realized. As one Participant put it:

> Without forensics you can't have these court proceedings therefore you can't help these people have closure in their life with something horrible that's occurred with them.

Helping victims find closure was a statement that resonated among all the Participants in the study. Contrary to what media portrayal might indicate, the mission of the forensic scientist is to present the evidence. One Participant quickly pointed out that being able to help exonerate the innocent and convict the guilty is not really the mission of the forensic scientist. If the court case is successful, meaning everything was presented accurately and the jury has intelligently arrived at a conclusion, then the forensic scientist knows that he has done a good job. That good job results in the victim finding closure leaving the forensic scientist feeling like he has done something positive for society and for others.

Listening to the Participants' accounts of how much satisfaction each gets from helping the victims, the community, and society it is the researcher's observation that of all job satisfaction aspects this one ranks highest. Participant 2 had a very satisfactory smile on her face when relaying that she has a sense of satisfaction knowing that she is doing public work and that she is helping bring justice to families. It is the researcher's summation that when it comes to forensic scientist job satisfaction experiences enhancing the lives of others far outweighs any other joys or benefits of the job. The overall feeling experienced by the researcher's is that what was important to the Participants was the victim. As one Participant sums up his experiences:

> If I have done my job to the best of my abilities at 100 or 110% capacity, I know that the product that I've released out to my client agencies, be that law enforcement or the district attorney's, I have helped a victim find closure.

MAJOR FINDINGS

The purpose of this phenomenological research study using qualitative methodology was to explore the lived job satisfaction experiences of eight forensic scientists to investigate whether their daily employment setting experiences play a role in job satisfaction. Participants for this research study were chosen using purposive sampling. Sproull (2002) defines purposive sampling as a nonrandom sampling technique that is indiscriminately done because the sample population contains characteristics that the researcher believes is important for the research area to be studied. Each Participant currently works within the field of forensic science as a forensic scientist. Individual one-on-one interviews were conducted. All interviews were audio taped and later transcribed. The use of audio taping was to ensure accuracy of the data during the analysis process.

The focal point of this study was on the research question: How do forensic scientists' daily employment setting experiences play a role in job satisfaction? This study explored whether such things as day-to-day tasks, unrealistic expectations, and the like affected the job satisfaction of forensic scientists. The forensic scientists discussed an indisputable devotion to their current job and to the field of forensic science. The interview question responses from the forensic scientists demonstrated that the Participants' day-to-day job experiences do not influence their overall job satisfaction. The essence of the Participants' words imply that such as with any job you have little daily tasks that may prove exasperating at times but those tasks are not enough to cause overall job dissatisfaction.

The principal essence the researcher got from the interviews is that the forensic scientists truly enjoy their jobs and could not even imagine being anything else besides a forensic scientist. Each Participant discussed the importance of their role in the forensic science process and how what they do changes the lives of the victims they serve. Taken as a whole, the feelings of each forensic scientist is that there is no other career they can picture themselves having and if they had it all to do over again they would still be a forensic scientist. Furthermore, Participants' overall thoughts were that the satisfaction of knowing they are contributing positively to the community and society with their skills and knowledge outweighs any negativity that daily tasks, unrealistic expectations, or media perceptions can add to their jobs.

To recap, the major finding of this study is that even with all the misconceptions, work demands, and other challenges the participating forensic scientists overall are in general satisfied with their jobs as forensic scientists. Consequently, this study also found in the course of researching for this study that forensic scientist research is severely deficient. Thus, any data that results from this research may provide some insight into the job experiences of forensic scientists. This scaled-down research study will optimistically be the catalyst for studies on a much larger scale in the future.

THE RESEARCH QUESTION

How do forensic scientists' daily employment setting experiences play a role in job satisfaction?

The recounted experiences of the Participants revealed that daily employment setting experiences does not play a role in job satisfaction. Participants noted that although daily tasks such as caseloads, fielding calls from officers or DA's, or menial tasks (washing spot plates, making solutions, and so on) may be tiresome, it does not make them dissatisfied with the job. The Participants view such tasks and any daily experiences as part of the job of being a forensic scientist. The overall picture of helping the victim or victims, community, and society mean more to them than daily annoyances. As one Participant divulged, there are many tasks that should be done by an assistant. But due to the fact that many agencies no longer employ students or assistants the analyst has to do whatever it takes to get the case done because there are bigger things involved and more important than the fact that one has to wash his own spot plate.

GOALS OF THE INTERVIEW QUESTIONS

INTERVIEW QUESTION 1

Question 1: What are some of the responsibilities required of your current position? How does this affect your overall views of the job?

The goal of this inquiry was to ascertain all the duties for which each Participant is responsible. Additionally, the inquiry wanted to ascertain if such duties affected their views of the job. Information from this inquiry assisted the researcher in learning the lived experiences of forensic scientist with regard to job satisfaction. Many of the Participants had multiple responsibilities that were related to their job title as well as duties that were not necessarily their responsibility but had to be done by someone.

Question 2: How accurate do you think the media (fictitious and mainstream) portrays what a forensic scientist does to get the job done? How does this portrayal affect your daily job?

This inquiry served two purposes for this study. The first goal of the inquiry was to get a first hand account of what the Participants thought about fictitious forensic scientists. The second goal of the inquiry was to give the Participants an opportunity to discuss how they are perceived in the media and to clear up any media myths with regard to forensic scientists and/or forensic science. Additionally, this inquiry wanted to elicit the Participants' lived experiences of how portrayals of the forensic scientist in print and video/television media affect their day-to-day jobs as forensic scientists. Overall, the Participants were in unison that how forensic science and forensic scientists are portrayed in the media is for the most part an inaccurate account.

Question 3: What are your thoughts with regard to fictitious forensic shows as to whether they help or hinder forensic science and the criminal justice process? How does it affect your daily job?

This inquiry served to elicit from the Participants whether or not the barrage of media on forensic science aid the field or does it a disservice. Additionally, the inquiry wanted to know what way, if any, fictitious media affects the Participants' daily job. The majority of the Participants agreed that although the attention to the field helps bring recognition it also brings some hindrances such as high expectations from the public and often law enforcement with regard to the capabilities of forensic science and forensic scientists.

Question 4: Compared to when you first started working as a forensic scientist would you say that you are as satisfied today as you were then?

This inquiry sought to have the Participants self-evaluate and determine whether or not their attitudes towards the job have changed since they began working in the field. There were varying responses from the Participants ranging from still satisfied to even more satisfied today than they were when they first entered the field.

Question 5: How have things changed both technologically and professionally in forensic science since you started in the field and how have these changes affected your job satisfaction outlook?

With this inquiry, the researcher wanted to get an idea of whether advancement in technology and the push for professionalism in the field of forensic science or lack thereof contributed to the Participants' job satisfaction. There were some disciplines, such as DNA, that benefit greatly from constant technological and standards update while other disciplines may not see technological advances quite so often.

Question 6: What are some of the things that contribute to your job satisfaction (e.g. pay, peers, management, and burnout)?

This direct inquiry sought to elicit straight forward responses from the Participants. This was the Participants' opportunity to simply name or list for the researcher what were the aspects of the job that made them pleased to come to work and be a forensic scientist. There were varying responses from the Participants as to what makes them satisfied with their status including the fact that peer relationships were healthy, supportive management, and simply the fact that they are giving back to the community.

Question 7: How do you feel about newcomers to the field? Do you feel they have unreasonable expectations about forensic science because of "TV forensics"? Does this make your job more difficult?

This inquiry further investigates the role, if any, media or TV forensics play in the Participants' daily work environment. Furthermore, the inquiry wanted to know the Participants' perception of new forensic scientists entering the field. Do new forensic scientists enter the field based on true forensic knowledge or were they steered into the field under false pretext? For example, did the "newbies" come into the field because of media forensics. Some of the responses from the Participants provided insight to an area not even considered by the researcher: some new entries into the field often have an ego or sense of entitlement and don't feel they have to start at the bottom or do grunge work.

Question 8: Has your work in forensics enhanced your life and the lives of others? Has this contributed to your job satisfaction?

The aim of this inquiry was to find out whether the Participants viewed their jobs as just another job or whether they saw themselves as contributors to a process that can result in a positive outcome. The overall responses from the Participants was that they viewed their jobs as forensic scientists as rewarding and they had a sense of pride knowing that they are giving back to the community and society by assisting those that need their help (victims).

Question 9: What do you feel can be done to promote forensic scientist job satisfaction, if any?

This inquiry gave the Participants one last chance to have their voices heard. Based on their current experiences the Participants provided some recommendations to management, those seeking to enter the field, and other suggestions of what works and what does not when it comes to the job of forensic scientist.

SUMMARY

Contained within Chapter Four was a synopsis of the findings, data collection and analysis for this research study on the lived experiences of forensic scientists as it relates to job satisfaction. Chapter Four also contained the Participants' verbatim responses to the Forensic Scientist Experiences Interview Guide. The in-depth interviews with the forensic scientists provided the researcher with useful information of the phenomena of job satisfaction among forensic scientists. The research wanted to explore the daily job experiences among a select group of forensic scientists to see how such experiences influenced job satisfaction.

The data received answered the research question of *'How do forensic scientists' daily employment setting experiences play a role in job satisfaction?'*. The research found that with this particular group of forensic scientists the daily tasks associated with their job experiences overall do not play a role in their job satisfaction or cause any type of job dissatisfaction. The Participants' experiences were analyzed using a modified version of Moustakas' van Kaam method. From the forensic scientist experiences data five core themes emerged. The five themes were (1) work affects the lives of others (2) unrealistic expectations from others; (3) constant comparison to TV forensics; (4) *CSI* Effect hinders job; and (5) job is satisfying.

The overall message extracted from the interviews is that the Participants are satisfied in their jobs as forensic scientists and that the daily tasks, no matter how numerous, does not even factor into any amount of dissatisfaction with the job. The researcher's interpretation was that the overall experience of helping victims or society far outweighed any negative experiences daily tasks might add to the job of being a forensic scientist.

Chapter Five will discuss results, conclusions, implications and recommendations for future research in forensic science with specific emphasis on the forensic scientist.

CHAPTER FIVE
RESULTS, CONCLUSIONS, AND RECOMMENDATIONS

INTRODUCTION

According to the American Academy of Forensic Sciences (2008), a forensic scientist is defined as an individual who uses scientific knowledge or applies science to the law to assist law enforcement, attorneys, courts, and others within the legal community. The purpose of this phenomenological qualitative research study using a modified version of Moustakas' van Kaam method with audio taped and transcribed structured one-on-one interviews was to explore the job satisfaction experiences of eight forensic scientists. The study was conducted to explore whether daily on the job experiences influenced job satisfaction. Chapter Five presents a discussion of the results, conclusions, implications and recommendations for future research with regard to forensic scientists and job satisfaction.

THE RESEARCH QUESTION

This qualitative phenomenological study was guided by the following research question:

How do forensic scientists' daily employment setting experiences play a role in job satisfaction?

Forensic scientists perform such tasks as report writing, dealing with the misinformed (law enforcement and attorneys who have TV ideologies about services), exasperating caseloads and so forth daily. The research question wanted to explore whether the many daily tasks that forensic scientists experience influenced job satisfaction experiences.

With this study, the researcher's wanted to give the uninformed and the misinformed a brief look into the lived experiences of forensic scientists. There are many misperceptions about forensic scientists as to who they are and what they do. Television and other media are the biggest perpetuators of the fallacies or half truths that exist about forensic scientists. The Participants' experiences will hopefully provide a little background into the day-to-day activities of real forensic sciences and what makes them satisfied or dissatisfied.

The data for this phenomenological study was obtained by means of one-on-one interviews with each Participant. Eight Participants total were interviewed for this phenomenological study. Due to the forensic scientist's having varying schedules or availability, the researcher met with each when it was most convenient for them. Each interview was no longer than 45 minutes. The Participants were forensic scientists from varying disciplines. There were forensic scientists from such disciplines as DNA, forensic chemistry, and firearms represented. Though the forensic scientists represented different disciplines, each had day-to-day duties that were similar as well as different due to duties that were discipline specific. Each Participant was provided an opportunity to review their transcribed interview to make certain that the researcher captured their words precisely.

Each forensic scientist's interview was audio recorded to make sure that the researcher accurately documented the interviewee's words. During the data analysis process the forensic scientists' responses were transcribed verbatim. The researcher then examined every statement that was relevant to the questions asked in the study. From this examination, recurring words and phrases emerged that allowed the researcher to categorize and create meaning units. These meaning units were an account of the researcher's understanding of the importance of the forensic scientist job satisfaction phenomena. Themes were then produced from the meaning units that developed from the data.

The results that were yielded from this study can not be generalized to all forensic scientists working in crime laboratories in the U. S. or around the world. This study's sample size was simply too small to make such a generalization. What this study desired was to speak with a few local forensic scientists to find out how they felt about their daily experiences working as a forensic scientist. In addition, it was this study's expectation that such a discussion would not only stimulate further research on forensic scientist job satisfaction but also stimulate research on other employment issues related to forensic personnel. The study of forensic scientists in the workplace is relatively new territory, compared to other law enforcement personnel, and research is much needed.

SUMMARY OF THEORETICAL PERSPECTIVE

There have been various theories used to guide research in the area of job satisfaction. Opponent process theory is one such theory. The fact that opponent process theory has been successfully applied in many different areas makes it generalizable to an area such as job satisfaction (Bowling, Beehr, Wagner, & Libkuman, 2005). As stated earlier in the study, there are three well-known theorists who have successfully explained job satisfaction: Edwin Locke in 1976 and Edward Lawler in 1973 with versions of what each termed discrepancy theory and Frank Landy in 1978 with his opponent process theory. After reviewing literature on these three theorists, as well as other job satisfaction theorists and theories, the theory selected to guide this study was Frank Landy's opponent process theory.

Landy (1978) devised his opponent process theory to explain how satisfied an individual was with a profession over time. Landy's opponent process theory was the best fit for this study to observe if job satisfaction experiences of forensic scientists changed over time even though the core duties of the job may not. The researcher's hypothesis for this study was that the job of forensic scientist may not have the exceptionally high or significant job satisfaction experience as perceived by many outside the field. The bulk of such perceptions people outside the field of criminal justice and forensic science acquire from media. The problem with much of the current media portrayal of forensic scientists is that many stray so far away from the truth that what remains is pure fiction. The outcome of this study was consistent with the Landy opponent process theory that supported this current study. Based on the perspectives of the Participants, the findings demonstrated that:

1. Forensic scientists are not experiencing the exceptionally high or extremely significant job satisfaction as the media depicts.
2. Over time, the satisfaction level of the forensic scientists generally remained consistent.
3. The satisfaction that the forensic scientist's get from the job has changed over time.

The results of this study not only supported the hypothesis regarding satisfaction experiences but it also confirmed that similar to other professions satisfaction with the job of forensic scientist does change after a while.

Landy's research in the area of job satisfaction revealed that for the average individual regardless of the work environment when it comes to the job, eventually people seem to show an unwavering or steady level of job satisfaction. Bhushan (2005) simplifies Landy's theory further by stating even though in the end the job may not change, the satisfaction that the individual gets from the job does change. All Participants in the study were in unison that job satisfaction levels are nowhere near the high levels that fictitious forensic scientists on television portray real life forensic scientists as possessing. Additionally, Participants in the study were quick to point out that the high job satisfaction viewed in the media is categorically not realistic.

As for the satisfaction one gets from the job, the forensic scientists in the study stated that satisfaction has without a doubt changed. Each Participant had varying reasons as to what satisfaction they got out of the job when they began their careers as forensic scientists (e.g. pay, status, or notoriety) compared to the satisfaction they currently get out of the job (e.g. advocates for justice or being a productive citizen). The Participants stated that these many years later what initially satisfied them has changed significantly. The consensus was that after years of working in the field they realized that the job of forensic scientists is not about them and the things that they get out of the job such as pay or recognition. The satisfaction that they get out of the job today is knowing that they are helping society and their immediate community by helping victims, exonerating the innocent, and assisting law enforcement in prosecuting the guilty.

SUMMARY OF RESULTS

According to a recent report by the California Crime Laboratory Review Task Force (2009), when it comes to retention of forensic scientists in crime laboratories across the state (California), some of the main reasons for unhappy forensic scientists include salary, lack of advancement opportunities, and burnout from heavy caseloads. The results of this study of forensic scientist who do work in a California crime lab demonstrated that the forensic scientists are satisfied with their jobs, salary, and other aspects of the job. There are many reasons why the California forensic scientists in this study expressed complete job satisfaction while the California Crime Laboratory Review Task Force had unsatisfied forensic scientists. Possibly what factors into such satisfaction is job location, management at this particular location, coworker relationships, size of the lab, and so forth. Or it could simply be that the California Crime Laboratory Review Task Force had a much larger sampling size and the majority of that sample was unsatisfied compared to the small sample size of this study where it turned out that all the Participants were satisfied with their jobs.

The purpose of this study was to comprehend the fundamental nature of what it truly means to work as a forensic scientist. This qualitative study used a one-on-one structured interview format to examine the daily lived experiences of forensic scientists to explore whether these daily experiences influenced job satisfaction experienced. This study demonstrated that the day-to-day job responsibilities that forensic scientists experience does not influence overall job satisfaction. Forensic scientists must not only on a daily basis deal with heavy caseloads but must also deal with attorneys, courts, other law enforcement entities and the like (Dowler, 2005; Sewell, 2006; Sheehan & Van Hasselt, 2003). In spite of all these responsibilities, the forensic scientists reported to the researcher that they still experience great satisfaction with the job because they know that all that they do is helping victims, the community, and society as a whole.

Although there is literature to support job satisfaction experiences of various other law enforcement personnel, literature to support forensic scientist in areas such as stress, job satisfaction and the like is practically non-existent.

CONCLUSIONS AS RELATED TO THE LITERATURE

The purpose of this study was to expand on the minimal, if not non-existent, literature available on forensic scientist job satisfaction. The results of this study provide new information to a literature base that is severely lacking in research when it comes to forensic scientist job satisfaction. Sewell (2000) illustrated that there has been research conducted in practically every area and subset of law enforcement but not forensic personnel. Job satisfaction among law enforcement personnel such as police officers, correctional officers, and so on has been well documented but again, not with forensic personnel. Not only is there a lack of literature on forensic scientist job satisfaction but there is also minimal to no research other than, as mentioned earlier, a few peer reviewed articles on forensic scientist stress or any other work related issues that forensic scientists may experience. The literature review showed that there is a definite need for research in this rapidly advancing area of law enforcement.

Research in various areas of criminal justice confirmed that members of corrections, police, probation, and other law enforcement personnel reported issues such as heavy caseloads, unrealistic deadlines, and low pay as some of the factors contributing to job satisfaction experiences (Castle, 2008; Childress et al, 1999; Dowler, 2005; Lambert & Hogan, 2009; Manzoni & Eisner, 2006; Sewell, 2006; Sheehan & Van Hasselt, 2003). The findings of this current study with forensic scientists are consistent with those studies that focused on the job satisfaction experiences of other law enforcement personnel. The Participants in this study reported experiencing similar challenges that their law enforcement cohorts experienced such as unrealistic deadlines, unrealistic expectations of the job of forensic scientist, and exceptionally heavy caseloads just to name a few.

The literature review for this study further demonstrated that the level of job satisfaction for an employee is very important because an unsatisfied employee could potentially result in an unproductive employee, an employee who has high work errors, and so on. Furthermore, the literature demonstrated that job satisfaction is a predictor of workplace issues such as burnout, high job turnover, absenteeism, and so forth (Castle, 2008; Dowler, 2005; Kohan & O'Connor, 2002; Wright & Bonett, 2007). The Participants in this study concurred with factors such as burnout possibly playing a role in poor job satisfaction. However, the Participants articulated how important it is to look at the bigger picture and not let such negative issues as burnout, high caseload, and the like affect their work product. The Participants further articulated that allowing such unconstructive attitudes towards the job into one's work practices could contribute to elevated work errors and this is unacceptable in the field of forensic science. Moreover, the Participants all affirmed that the primary factor that keeps them satisfied with their status and what keeps them from allowing negativity to set in is the fact that they are giving back to the community and helping society as a whole. Lastly, the Participants communicated that forensic scientists are directly influencing an individual's life and even though there may be aspects of the job or days that may make the job less satisfying than others helping victims takes precedence over what the forensic scientist may be experiencing.

As indicated in the literature reviewed, the field of forensic science has experienced rapid growth compared to other areas of law enforcement due to intense media interest (Finneran, 2003; Minn, 2009; Robbers, 2008; Willing, 2004).

The Participants in the current study were in accord with the literature that indeed presently, there is vast interest in the field and the popularity of such media to some extent played a role in their daily work experiences. The forensic scientists in the study described such attention as a double-edged sword. On one hand, the attention brings awareness of the field and gives insight to the masses, in particular those who did not even know that the field existed. On the other hand, the forensic scientists communicated to the researcher that such attention does a disservice to the field in that the bulk of what is displayed is usually a misrepresentation of forensic scientists, forensic science, and the field's capabilities, which leads to huge misperceptions. The latter revelation by the Participants is consistent with what was discovered during the literature review. That discovery was that in spite of the fact that fabricated forensic shows bring consciousness to the field the bulk of the existing forensic science shows often present forensic science in a very impractical light and the line between fiction and reality are often distorted (Goode, 2004; Houck, 2006; Shelton, 2008; Tesler, 2010; Williams, Rickard, & Fisher, 2005).

The Chapter Two literature review demonstrated that there is a critical need for research in the area of job satisfaction and forensic science. According to Dowler (2005), there is an overabundance of literature on other law enforcement personnel and job satisfaction. According to the literature reviewed, there is well over 30 years of research on police, corrections, probation, and other law enforcement personnel that even include entry level personnel such as support staff. However, literature on forensic scientists and its personnel is nominal to absent. The Participants in the study acknowledged that there are a few technical articles here and there but many of the Participants stated they had yet to see any in-depth research on forensic scientists. The insufficient amount of research on forensic scientists and other forensic personnel is an obvious indication that these are areas in desperate need of research. The researcher's are optimistic that this study has contributed to the gap in the rather inadequate forensic personnel literature database.

LIMITATIONS OF THE STUDY

As previously discussed, there is no way that the results from this small-scale research can be generalized to all forensic scientists working for all agencies in existence. One reason a generalization cannot be made is that the data collected via purposive sampling for this research originated from only eight forensic scientists, which is not a large enough sample size or data to conclude that all forensic scientists share these ideas. According to Creswell (2003), when a purposive sampling technique is used it decreases the researcher's ability to generalize the findings. To gain a better knowledge of how forensic scientists as a whole feel about the nature of their jobs a much wider sample base must be acquired for research.

Another reason the results of this study cannot be generalized is because the data gathered for this study was collected from forensic scientists at one specific

laboratory. Participants working at other laboratories that are larger, in the same or different city, county, or system may report different job satisfaction experiences.
When this research began, the following limitations were anticipated:
- Due to the small number of forensic scientists interviewed, the results could not be generalized to all other agencies or forensic scientists.
- Forensic scientists not being honest with their answers could produce results that were inaccurate.
- Due to daily time constraints and heavy work caseloads, forensic scientists could be rapid in their responses and not give the interview time serious attention, as they could possibly be more concerned with getting back to work.
- Some Participants could have second thoughts about participating in the study and thus may not be as forthright with responses.
- There could be underlying factors that contribute to the forensic scientists' job satisfaction other than the factors associated with the job.

Here is how each limitation actually affected the outcome of the study:
- *Due to the small number of forensic scientists interviewed, the results could not be generalized to all other agencies or forensic scientists.*

    As previously discussed, this study cannot be generalized to all agencies or all forensic scientists in existence due to the sample size.
- *Forensic scientists not being honest with their answers could produce results that were inaccurate.*

    Once the interviews commenced, by the verbal and nonverbal cues of the Participants displayed the researcher believes that all answers were being honestly given. Thus the researcher is confident in the accuracy of the study's results based on the data collected.
- *Due to daily time constraints and heavy work caseloads, forensic scientists could be rapid in their responses and not give the interview time serious attention, as they could possibly be more concerned with getting back to work.*

    This was not an issue. Each Participant completed the interviews without even thinking "Oh, we have to hurry so I can get back to work". Participants took their time and really analyzed the questions prior to answering. Participants did not seem hurried in their responses.
- *Some Participants could have second thoughts about participating in the study and thus may not be as forthright with responses.*

    All Participants were as happy to participate at the day and time of the interview as they were when they were initially asked to participate in the study. Participants were even more elated on the interview day because they were anxious to have their voices heard and were excited that they were asked to participate.
- *There could be underlying factors that contribute to the forensic scientists' job satisfaction other than the factors associated with the job.*

Many of the Participants expressed that what contributed to their job satisfaction had nothing to do with factors such as salary, coworkers, or management. Overall, the thought of helping victims, the community, and society were underlying factors that contributed to their job satisfaction. Also, having a positive life and other outlets outside of work (family, friends, and hobbies) is what brought the Participants great joy and thus contributed to their job satisfaction. As one Participant explained, he has found that with all his many years of work experience those individuals in the workplace who are always negative and unhappy at work has nothing going on outside the workplace or has a negative and unhappy life at home.

Although the aforementioned limitations did not prove problematic for the researcher's, the researcher's did think of two particular limitations that could have potentially played a role in the current study. The researcher's did not think that such occurred but there is always that possibility because there are some people who are extremely good at masking their behavior. The researcher's wondered if 1) could the use of an audio recorder have influenced the Participants' responses and 2) although the Participants are listed anonymously did fear of being identified if in the future someone reads the dissertation play a role in the responses. Again, the researcher's got an overall feeling that the Participants were being forthright in their answers however; in research there always exists the possibility that Participants do not fully disclose, lie, or simply tell the researcher what they think the researcher wants to hear.

The last possible limitation to the study could be the decision to use qualitative methodology. Quantitative research methodologies typically provide the researcher with methods such as surveys, questionnaires, longitudinal, cross-sectional, experimental, or quasi-experimental options to investigate a phenomenon. Qualitative research methodologies also provide the researcher several methods of measurement however, qualitative methodologies utilize methods such as interviews, focus groups, or case studies to capture the Participant's lived experiences. In other words, quantitative methodology results in data that is in numerical form whereas qualitative methods produce data that consists of words or thoughts. Since qualitative methodology does not produce numerical results, qualitative research can be viewed as limiting because the data and findings can be subject to the interpretation of the researcher or individual viewing it.

SIGNIFICANCE OF THE STUDY

The information resulting from this research will be a small contribution to the gap in the forensic science literature in the area of job satisfaction as it relates to forensic scientists. The responses given by the Participants in this study could be utilized by forensic organizations as a reference tool to investigate job satisfaction among their forensic scientists. The voices of the forensic scientists in this study represent the voices of many, not all, forensic scientists working within the field of forensic science. This study will give those unfamiliar or misinformed about forensic scientist a glimpse into the daily life of a forensic scientist.

The Participants in this study, real life forensic scientists, experience real issues that go beyond the perceived glitz and glamour that is portrayed in the media. The forensic scientists in this study acknowledged that there are aspects of the job that could potentially cause poor job satisfaction among forensic scientists. Forensic science organizations could use such information to minimize or eliminate negative aspects in their forensic scientists' daily experiences. Identifying aspects of the job that forensic scientists are dissatisfied with could assist forensic science organizations in assessing how or what can be done to improve poor job satisfaction in the workplace.

IMPLICATIONS AND FUTURE RECOMMENDATIONS

STUDY'S CONTRIBUTION TO THE LITERATURE BASE

This phenomenological inquiry provided an opportunity for forensic scientists to give individuals outside the field a glance into the real work experiences of forensic scientists. Information on the experiences of forensic scientists (stress, job satisfaction, and other physical or psychological issues) could not be located during the extensive review of the literature for this study. The Participants in the study were encouraged to speak candidly about various aspects of their jobs as forensic scientists. The information resulting from these very open conversations will be a valuable contribution to the insufficient literature base that exists on forensic scientists.

This current study's review of the literature found that sub-specialties of law enforcement, particularly forensic science, lack research in quantitative as well as qualitative research (National Research Center, 2009; Sewell, 2000). The research data as well as results acquired by this study will be a springboard to filling the huge gap that exists in forensic scientist research. All information revealed during this study can give managers of crime laboratories an understanding of what forensic scientists are experiencing and thus aid them in identifying what experiences may potentially make their forensic scientists unsatisfied with their jobs. It is furthermore anticipated that this research will stimulate future research interest in not only the area of forensic science but also further study in forensic scientist job satisfaction, exploration of forensic scientist stress, as well as all other potential occupational issues for which forensic scientists may most likely be susceptible.

IMPLICATIONS

Forensic scientists must not only on a daily basis deal with heavy caseloads but must also deal with attorneys, courts, other law enforcement entities and the like

(Dowler, 2005; Sewell, 2006; Sheehan & Van Hasselt, 2003). This research study examined the daily lived experiences of eight forensic scientists working within a crime laboratory setting. The findings suggest that the day-to-day job responsibilities that forensic scientists experience does not influence overall job satisfaction.

Implications of this study are that forensic scientists may not be experiencing the significantly high job satisfaction that is alluded to in the media, but forensic scientists do experience some level of job satisfaction. Further implications are that what yields satisfaction to the forensic scientists are not necessarily the aspects of the job or salary but the joy of helping victims, the community, and society are what yields job satisfaction. This study discovered that forensic scientists have a lot to say with regard to their experiences, the needs of the forensic scientist, and so on and they would like their voices to be heard. The study of forensic scientists' well-being in the workplace is an unexploited area of potential and much needed research.

FUTURE RECOMMENDATIONS

As noted several times throughout this study, there are decades of research as it relates to the job satisfaction experiences of correctional officers, police officers, and other law enforcement personnel (Dowler, 2005). However, review of existing research demonstrated research on forensic science and forensic personnel is severely deficient. There are many possible reasons for this research deficiency in the area of forensic science. One major reason for the deficiency could be lack of funding for research.

According to the Committee of Identifying the Needs of the Forensic Sciences Community, National Research Council (2009), research in forensic science is not well supported with funding compared to other disciplines. This is a major limiting factor because not being able to find funding to support research stifles the field. In order for the field to stay current in the U. S., conducting research is a must in order for the forensic science discipline to advance as well as be comparable to other countries. It is strongly recommended that forensic organizations seek ways to obtain grants and other monies that will help advance continued research in forensic science.

If agencies can secure grants for research similar to grants like the Coverdell grant, then research in forensic science would make a significant breakthrough. Briefly, the Paul Coverdell Forensic Science Improvement Grants Program awards grants to both state and local agencies to assist in improving the quality and timeliness of forensic science (NIJ, 2012). Many agencies use such grant to cover forensic scientist overtime so that case backlogs can be eliminated. The grant can also be used to fund forensic scientists' training, conference attendances, laboratory equipment, supplies, and even allows for the hiring of forensic personnel as needed to eliminate case backlogs. Having grants like the Coverdell grant but for conducting research would be a step in the right direction to bring forensic science up to the levels of research in other law enforcement disciplines.

Another recommendation for future exploration is that of finding ways to encourage forensic scientists to conduct research in the field. Agencies must encourage and allow their forensic scientist to conduct research. Who is better at exploring the lived experiences of forensic personnel than forensic personnel? In addition to the other recommendations, future research should also include study of occupational issues for other forensic personnel such as crime scene responders, forensic nurses, evidence technicians, and so forth.

Lastly, based on literature review of law enforcement studies using various methodologies to research job satisfaction, it appeared that there has been success using quantitative as well as qualitative methodologies. This study used qualitative methodologies and although it makes a small contribution to the literature base further research on this particular topic is needed. It is recommended that a replication of this study be conducted using a larger population and quantitative methodology to gain knowledge as to the actual number of forensic scientists experiencing job satisfaction. If qualitative methodology is used again perhaps Participants working at laboratories that are larger, in a different city, county, or system should be used as they may report different job satisfaction experiences. Again, for both methodologies it is recommended that a larger sample size be used.

Future research with regard to forensic scientist job satisfaction could also widen to compare and contrast the satisfaction levels of forensic scientists from different disciplines (e.g. Questioned Documents, Trace Evidence, Toxicology and so on) to determine if one discipline experiences more satisfaction than another. Another potential area of research could even include how the *CSI* Effect factors into the daily lived job satisfaction experiences of forensic scientists. As one can see and as stated earlier, the field of forensic science has many areas of research opportunities. The only thing needed is researchers willing to take on the daunting task or researching. Gathering data should not be an issue because there are forensic scientists who are ready and willing to provide any information a researcher may want or need. They are just waiting for someone to approach them and ask them to share their thoughts just as this study did.

REFERENCES

Almirall, J. R., & Furton, K. G. (2003). Trends in forensic science education: Expansion and increased accountability. *Analytical and Bioanalytical Chemistry, 376*(8), 1156-1159. doi:10.1007/s00216-003-1891-4.

American Academy of Forensic Sciences. (2008). *Welcome to the fascinating world of forensic science.* Retrieved from http://www.aafs.org/default.asp?section_id=resources&page_id=choosing_a_career#Bokmark1.

American Psychological Association Media Room. (2007). *Stress tip sheet.* Retrieved from http://apahelpcenter.mediaroom.com/index.php?s=page A& item=42.

American Psychological Association. (2011). *Stress: The different kinds of stress.* Retrieved from http://www.apa.org/helpcenter/stress-kinds.aspx.

American Society of Crime Laboratory Directors. (n.d.). *Welcome to ASCLD.* Retrieved from http://ascld.org/content/welcome-ascld.

Aspers, P. (2004). *Empirical Phenomenology: An approach for qualitative research.* Retrieved from http://www2.lse.ac.uk/methodologyInstitute/pdf/Qual Papers/Aspers-Patrik-Phenomenology04.pdf.

Barbara, J. J. (2008). Point of view: Ethical practices in forensics. *Forensic Magazine.* Retrieved from http://www.forensicmag.com/articles.asp?pid=217.

Bassett, C. (2006). Beyond *CSI*: Careers in forensic science. *Medical Laboratory Observer, 28.*

Becker, W. S. & Dale, W. M. (2007). Critical human resource issues: Scientists under pressure. *Forensic Science Communication, 9*(2), 1-11.

Bhushan, A. (2005). *Theory and measurement for job satisfaction.* Retrieved from http://www.businessandlaw.com/articles/human_resources/theory_and_mea surement_for_job_satisfaction.

Boke, K & Nalla, M. K. (2009). Police organizational culture and job satisfaction: A comparison of law enforcement officers' perceptions in two Midwestern states in the U. S. *Journal of Criminal Justice and Security, 1*, 55-73.

Bowling, N. A., Beehr, T. A., Wagner, S. H., & Libkuman, T. M. (2005). Adaptation-level theory, opponent process theory, and dispositions: An integrated approach to the stability of job satisfaction. *Journal of Applied Psychology, 90*(6), 1044-1053.

Brody, D. C., DeMarco, C., & Lovrich, N. P. (2002). Community policing and job satisfaction: Suggestive evidence of positive workforce effects from a multijurisdictional comparison in Washington State. *Police Quarterly, 5*(2), 181-205. doi:10.1177/1098611102129198093.

Brough, P. (2004). Comparing the influence of traumatic and organizational stressors on the psychological health of police, fire, and ambulance officers. *International Journal of Stress Management, 11*(3), 227-244. doi: 10.1037/1072-5245.11.3.227.

Brough, P. & Frame, R. (2004). Predicting police job satisfaction and turnover intentions: The role of social support and police organizational variables. *New Zealand Journal of Psychology, 33,* 8-18.

Burke, T. W. (1995). Dispatcher stress. *FBI Law Enforcement Bulletin, 64*(10), 1-6.

Burke, T. W. (2001). *The relationship between dispatcher stress and social support, job satisfaction, and locus-of-control.* (Volumes I and II) (Doctoral dissertation). Retrieved from ProQuest Dissertations and Theses database. (9130298).

California Crime Laboratory Review Task Force. (2009). An examination of forensic science in California. *California Department of Justice Office of the Attorney General Publication,* 1-181.

Campbell, A. (2007). *The myth of CSI: Is forensic science the panacea of justice.* Retrieved from http://www.the-csi-effect.com/.

Castillo, J. X. & Cano, J. (2004). Factors explaining job satisfaction among faculty. *Journal of Agricultural Education, 45*(3), 65-74.

Castle, T. L. (2008). Satisfied in the jail?: Exploring the predictors of job satisfaction among jail officers. *Criminal Justice Review, 33*(1), 48-63. doi:10.1177/0734016808315586.

Caudill, D. S. (2008). Idealized images of science and law: The expert witness in trial movies. *St. John's Law Review, 82,* 921-949.

Childress, R. Talucci, V., & Wood, J. (1999). Fighting the enemy within: Helping officers deal with stress. *Corrections Today, 61*(7), 70-72.

Council on Forensic Science Education. (n.d.). Retrieved from http://www.criminology.fsu.edu/COFSE/default.html.

Creswell, J. (2003). *Research design: Qualitative, quantitative, and mixed methods approach* (second edition). Thousand Oaks, CA: Sage Publications.

CSI experts showcase latest forensic technology tools. (2007). In *Forensic Magazine.* Retrieved from http://www.forensicmag.com/News_Articles.asp?pid=182.

Curran, S. F. (2003). Separating fact from fiction about police stress. *Behavioral Health Management,* 38-40.

Dantzker, M. L. (1997). Police officer job satisfaction: Does agency size make a difference? *Criminal Justice Policy Review, 8*(2-3), 309-322. doi: 10.1177/088740349700800209.

Desio, P. J., Gaensslen, R. E., & Lee, H. C. (1985). Undergraduate education in forensic science and chemistry. *Journal of Chemical Education, 62*(12), p1053. doi:10.1021/ed062p1053.

Doak, S. & Assimakopoulos, D. (2007). How do forensic scientists learn to become competent in casework reporting in practice: A theoretical and empirical approach. *Forensic Science International, 167*, 201-206.

Dowler, K. (2005). Job satisfaction, burnout, and perception of unfair treatment: The relationship between race and police work. *Police Quarterly, 8*(4), 476-489. doi:10.1177/1098611104269787.

Dowler, K., Fleming, T., & Muzzatti, S. L. (2006). Constructing crime: Media, crime, and popular culture. *Canadian Journal of Criminology and Criminal Justice, 48*(6), 837-850. doi:10.3138/cjccj.48.6.837.

Education. (2007). In *FBI Law Enforcement Bulletin, 76*(12), 27-27.

Erzinclioglu, Z. (2004). *The illustrated guide to forensics: True crime scene investigations.* New York, NY: Carlton Publishing Group/Barnes & Noble Books.

Finn, P. (1997). Reducing stress: An organization-centered approach. *FBI Law Enforcement Bulletin, 66*(8).

Finneran, K. (2003). Prime time science. *Science & Technology, 20*(1), 23-23.

Flood, A. (2010). Understanding phenomenology. *Nurse Researcher, 17*(2), 7-15.

Garcia, L., Nesbary, D. K., & Gu, J. (2004). Perceptual variations of stressors among police officers during an era of decreasing crime. *Journal of Contemporary Criminal Justice, 2*(1), 33-50. doi:10.1177/1043986203262300.

Goode, E. (2004). The skeptic meets *CSI* (Crime Scene Investigation): How far should artistic license go? *Skeptic, 10*(4), 75-77.

Greene, J. R. (1989). Police officer job satisfaction and community perceptions: Implications for community-oriented policing. *Journal of Research in Crime and Delinquency, 26*(2), 168-183. doi:10.1177/0022427889026002004.

Gurbuz, A. (2007). An assessment on the effect of educational level on the job satisfaction from the tourism sector point of view. *Dogus University Journal, 8*(1), 36-46.

Harpold, J. A. & Feemster, J. D. (2002). Negative influences of police stress. *FBI Law Enforcement Bulletin, 71*(9), 1-6.

Hilton, O. (1993). *Scientific examination of questioned documents: Revised Edition.* Boca Raton, FL: CRC Press.

Houck, M. M. (2006). *CSI*: Reality. *Scientific American, 295*(1), 85-89. doi: 10.1038/scientificamerican0706-84.

Hyman, O. (2004). Perceived social support and symptoms of secondary traumatic stress in disaster workers. *Journal of Traumatic Stress, 17*(2), 149-156.

International Organization for Standardization. (2009). *About ISO.* Retrieved from http://www.iso.org/iso/about.htm.

Job Satisfaction. (2011). In *BusinessDictionary.com.* Retrieved from http://www.businessdictionary.com/definition/job-satisfaction.html.

Jones, A. (2009). *Education requirements for forensic science*. Retrieved from http://www.ehow.com/about_5426312_education-requirements-forensic-science.html.

Kenny, D. T. & Cooper, C. L. (2003). Introduction: Occupational stress and its management. *International Journal of Stress Management, 10*(4), 275-279.

Kirk-Brown, A. & Wallace, D. (2004). Predicting burnout and job satisfaction in workplace counselors: The influence of role stressors, job challenge, and organizational knowledge. *Journal of employment Counseling, 41*, 29-37.

Kleck, G., Tark, J., & Bellows, J. J. (2006). What methods are most frequently used in research in criminology and criminal justice? *Journal of Criminal Justice, 34*, 147-152.

Kohan, A. & O'Connor, B. P. (2002). Police officer job satisfaction in relation to mood, well-being, and alcohol consumption. *The Journal of Psychology, 136*(3), 307-318.

Kruse, C. (2010). Producing absolute truth: *CSI* science is wishful thinking. *American Anthropologist, 112*(1), 79-91. doi:10.1111/j.1548-1433.2009.v 01198.x

Lambert, E. & Hogan, N. (2009). The importance of job satisfaction and organizational commitment in shaping turnover intent: A test of a causal model. *Criminal Justice Review, 34*(1), 96-118. doi:10.1177/073401680 8324230.

Landy, F. J. (1978). An opponent process theory of job satisfaction. *Journal of Applied Psychology, 63*(5), 533-547.

Lawler, E. E. (1973). *Motivation in work organizations*. Monterey, CA: Brooks/Cole.

Lee, W. J., Phelps, J. R, & Beto, D. R. (2009). Turnover intention among probation officers and direct care staff. *Federal Probation, 73*(3), 28-39.

Leedy, P. D., & Ormrod, J. E. (2005). *Practical research: Planning and design.* (eighth edition). Upper Saddle River, NJ: Pearson Merrill/Prentice Hall.

Lyons, D. (2006). Capturing DNA's crime-fighting potential. *State Legislatures*, pp.16-17. Retrieved from http://www.thefreelibrary.com/Capturing+DNA's +crime+fighting+potential%3A+DNA+databases+are+expanding...-a0142923268.

Mann, M. (2006). The "*CSI* Effect": Better jurors through television and science?. *Buffalo Public Interest Law Journal, 42*, 157-183.

Manzoni, P. & Eisner, M. (2006). Violence between police and public: Influences of work related stress, job satisfaction, burnout, and situational factors. *Criminal Justice and Behavior, 33*(5), 613-645. doi:10.1177/00938548062 88039.

Mayo Clinic. (2007). *Stress symptoms: Effects on your body, feelings and behavior.* Retrieved from http://www.mayoclinic.com/health/stresssymptoms/SR00 008_D.

McDonald, A. F. (2008). *A CSI effect investigation: Media, curiosity, and the pursuit of closure* (Doctoral dissertation). Retrieved from ProQuest Dissertations and Theses database. (1460866).

Mennell, J. & Shaw, I. (2006). The future of forensic and crime scene science, Part I. A UK forensic science user and provider perspective. *Forensic Science International, 157*(1), 7-12. doi:10.1016/j.forsciint.2005.12.022.

Mertens, D.M. (2005). *Research and evaluation in education and psychology integrating diversity with quantitative, qualitative, and mixed methods* (second edition). Thousand Oaks, CA: Sage Publications.

Millen, P. (2000). Is crime scene investigation forensic science? Are crime scene investigators forensic scientists? *Science & Justice, 40*(2), 125-126.

Miller, H. A., Mire, S., & Kim, B. (2009). Predictors of job satisfaction among police officers: Does personality matter? *Journal of Criminal Justice, 37*, 419-426. doi:10.1016/j.jcrimjus.2009.07.001.

Minn, T. (2009). The *CSI* Effect: Real life crime investigators say it isn't as easy as it looks on *CSI*. *Inland Empire Magazine, 34*(3), 78-83.

Mire, S. (2005). *Correlates of job satisfaction among police officers* (Doctoral dissertation). Retrieved from ProQuest Dissertations and Theses database. (3190117).

Mopas, M. (2007). Examining the "*CSI* effect" through an ant lens. *Crime Media Culture, 3*(1), 110-117. doi:10.1177/1741659007074455.

Moustakas, C. (1994). *Phenomenological research methods*. Thousand Oaks, CA: Sage Publications.

Murphy, E. (2007). The new forensics: Criminal justice, false certainty, and the second generation of scientific evidence. *California Law Review, 95*, 721-797.

National Institute of Justice. (2007). Helping probation and parole officers cope with stress. *Corrections Today, 69*(1), 70-71.

National Institute of Justice. (2012). Coverdell Forensic Science Improvement Grants Program. Retrieved from http://www.nij.gov/topics/forensics/lab-operations/capacity/nfsia/welcome.htm.

National Institute for Occupational Safety and Health. (1999a). *Stress*. Retrieved from http://www.cdc.gov/niosh/atwork.html.

National Institute for Occupational Safety and Health. (1999b). *Stress...At work*. Retrieved from http://www.cdc.gov/niosh/docs/99-101/.

National Research Council. (2009). *Strengthening forensic science in the United States: A path forward*. Washington, DC: National Academic Press.

National Women's Health Resource Center (2002). *Stress*. Retrieved from http://www.healthywomen.org/healthtopics/stress#.

The nature and causes of job satisfaction (1976). In M. Dunnette (Ed.), *Handbook of industrial and organizational psychology* (pp. 1297-1349). Chicago, IL: Rand McNally.

Neuman, W. L. (2003). *Social research methods: Qualitative and quantitative approaches* (fifth edition). Boston, MA: Pearson Education.

O'Connor, T. (2006). *Police stress and Employee Assistance Programs.* Retrieved from http://www.apsu.edu/oconnort/4000/4000lect05.htm.

Perron, B. E. & Hiltz, B. S. (2006). Burnout and secondary trauma among forensic interviewers of abused children. *Child and Adolescent Social Work Journal, 23*(2), 216-234. doi:10.1007/s10560-005-0044-3.

Pietersen, C. (2005). Job satisfaction of hospital nursing staff. *Journal of Human Resource Management, 3*(2), 19-25.

Postrel, V. (2007). Beautiful minds. *The Atlantic Monthly, 300*(2), 1-2. Retrieved from http://www.theatlantic.com/doc/200709/csi.

Ramsland, K. (2009). The facts about fiction: What Grissom could learn about forensic psychology. *The Journal of Psychiatry & Law, 37* (1), 37-50.

Richardson, A., M., Burke, R. J., & Martinussen, M. (2006). Work and health outcomes among police officers: The mediating role of police cynicism and engagement. *International Journal of Stress Management, 13*(4), 555-574. doi:10.1037/1072-5245.13.4.555.

Rincon, P. (2005). *CSI* shows give 'unrealistic view'. [Electronic version]. *BBC News, Science/Nature.*

Robbers, M. L. P. (2008). Blinded by science: The social construction of reality in forensic television shows and its effect on criminal jury trials. *Criminal Justice Policy Review, 19*(1), 84-102. doi:10.1177/0887403407305982.

Rodes, J. C. (2005). Job satisfaction and life satisfaction revisited: A longitudinal test of an integrated model. *Human Relations, 57*(9), 1205-1230. doi:10.1177/0018726704047143.

Rudin, N. & Inman, K. (2002). *Forensic science timeline.* Retrieved from http://www.forensicdna.com/Timeline020702.pdf.

Rush, G. E. (2000). *The dictionary of criminal justice* (fifth edition). Dushkin/McGraw-Hill.

Saari, L. M. & Judge, T. A. (2004). Employee attitudes and job satisfaction. *Human Resource Management, 43*(4), 395-407.

Saferstein, R. (1982). *Forensic science handbook.* Englewood Cliffs, NJ: Prentice Hall/Regents.

Saferstein, R. (2004). *Forensic science handbook (Vol II)* (second edition). Englewood Cliffs, NJ: Prentice Hall.

Santa-Barbara, J. & Shain, M. (1999). When workplace stress stifles productivity. *Drake Business Review, 1*(1), p27-29.

Sappenfield, M. & Goodale, G. (2003). From Lindbergh to Laci, a growing forensics fancy. *Christian Science Monitor, 95*(104), 1. Retrieved from http://www.csmonitor.com/2003/0424/p01s01-ussc.html.

Schweitzer, N. J. & Saks, M. J. (2007). The *CSI* Effect: Popular fiction about forensic science affects the public's expectations about real forensic science. *Jurimetrics Journal, 47,* 357-364.

Science in Court. (2010). In *Nature, 464*(7287), 325. doi:10.1038/464325a.

Scott, E. (2005). *Acute stress.* Retrieved from http://stress.about.com/od/stressmanagementglossary/g/accutestress.htm.

Sewell, J. D. (2000). Identifying and mitigating workplace stress among forensic laboratory managers. *Forensic Science Communications, 2* (2), 1-9.

Sewell, J. D. (2006). Dealing with employee stress: How managers can help or hinder their personnel. *FBI Law Enforcement Bulletin, 75*, 1-6.

Sheehan, D. C. & Van Hasselt, V. B. (2003). Identifying law enforcement stress reactions early. *FBI Law Enforcement Bulletin, 72*, 12-17.

Shelton, D. E. (2008). The *CSI* Effect: Does it really exist? *National Institute of Justice Journal, 259.*

Sims, B., Ruiz, J., Weaver, G., and Harvey, W. L. (2005). Police perceptions of their working environment: Surveying the small department. *International Journal of Police Science and Management, 7*(4), 245-263.

Solomon, R. L. & Corbit, J. D. (1973). An opponent-process theory of motivation: Temporal dynamics of affect. *Psychological Review, 81,* 119-145.

Spector, P. E. (1985). Measurement of human service staff satisfaction: Development of the Job Satisfaction Survey. *American Journal of Community Psychology, 13*, 693-713.

Spector, P. E. (1997). *Job satisfaction: Application, assessment, causes, and consequences.* Thousand Oaks, CA: SAGE Publications.

Sproull, N. L. (2002). *Handbook of research methods: A guide for practitioners and students in the social sciences* (second edition). Lanham, MD: Scarecrow Press.

Stankiewicz, H. (2007). Investigating the worldwide popularity of forensics. *Pell Scholars and Senior Theses.* (Paper 12). Retrieved from http://www.escholar.salve.edu/cgi/viewcontent.cgi?article=1012&context=pell_theses.

Stinchcomb, J. B. (2004). Searching for stress in all the wrong places: Combating chronic organizational stressors in policing. *Police Practice and Research, 5*(3), 259-277. doi:10.1080/156142604200227594.

Stress. (2005). In *Encarta Webster's College Dictionary* (second edition). New York, NY: Boomsbury Publications.

Stress. (2008). In *HealthyWomen.org*. Retrieved from http://www.healthywomen.org/condition/stress.

Stress. (2009). In *Merriam-Webster's Online Medical Dictionary.* Retrieved from http://www.merriam-webster.com/medical/stress.

Sykes, D., Holland, M., & Shaler, R. (2006). Forensic science education: Designing an effective curriculum. *Forensic Magazine* http://www.forensicmag.com/article/forensic-science-education-designing-effective-curriculum?page=0,0.

Tesler, P. (2010). Shadows of doubt. *CSI* science isn't as solid as the TV shows lead us to believe. *Current Science, 95*(9), 8-9.

Toobin, J. (2007). The *CSI* Effect. *New Yorker, 83*(11), 30-35. Retrieved from http://www.newyorker.com/reporting/2007/05/07/070507fa_fact_toobin.

Torpy, J. M., Lynm, C., & Glass, R. M. (2007). Chronic stress and the heart. *The Journal of the American Medical Association, 298*(14), 1722. doi:10.1001/jama.298.14.1722.

Trochim, W. M. K. (2006). *Qualitative validity. Research methods knowledge base*. Retrieved from http://www.socialresearchmethods.net/kb/qualval.php.

U. S. Department of Justice/Office of Justice Programs/National Institute of Justice. (2007). *Forensic Sciences: Review of status and needs—Issues and practices*. Retrieved from http://www.ncjrs.gov/pdffiles1/173412.pdf.

Vargas-Perez, H., Ting-A-Kee, R. A., Heinmiller, A., Sturgess, J. E., van der Kooy, D. (2007). A test of opponent process theory of motivation using lesions that selectively block morphine rewards. *European Journal of Neuroscience, 25*, 3713-3718.

Warrington, D. (2008). Who says you can't do that? Gadgets. *Forensic Magazine*. Retrieved from http://www.forensicmag.com/articles.asp?pid=195.

Wells, D. T. (2003). Reducing stress for officers and their families. *Corrections Today, 65*(2), 24-25.

White, J. W., Lawrence, P. S., Biggerstaff, C., & Grubb, T. D. (1985). Factors of stress among police officers. *Criminal Justice and Behavior, 12*(1), 111-128. doi:10.1177/0093854885012001008.

Williams, R. (Presenter), Rickard, P., & Fisher, D. (Producers). (2005, April 9). *The Science Show: The truth about CSI (ABC Radio National)* [Transcript] Australia: Australian Broadcasting Corporation. Retrieved from http://www.abc.net.au/cgibin/common/printfriendly.pl?http://www.abc.net.au/rn/science/ss/stories/s1339511.htm.

Willing, R. (2004). "*CSI* effect" has juries wanting more evidence. *USA Today*, Retrieved from http://www.usatoday.com/news/nation/2004-08-05-csi-effect_x.htm.

Wojnar, D. M. & Swanson, K. M. (2007). Phenomenology: An exploration. *Journal of Holistic Nursing, 25*(3), 172-180. doi:10.1177/0898010106295172.

Wright, T. A. & Bonett, D. G. (2007). Job satisfaction and psychological well-being as nonadditive predictors of workplace turnover. *Journal of Management, 33*(2), 141-160. doi: 10.1177/0149206306297582.

Zhao, J., He, N., & Lovrich, N. (2002). Predicting five dimensions of police officer stress: Looking more deeply into organizational settings for sources of police stress. *Police Quarterly, 5*(1), 43-62. doi:10.1177/109861110200500103.

INDEX

American Academy of Forensic Sciences (AAFS), 1–3, 7, 24–25, 61
American Society of Crime Laboratory Directors (ASCLD), 3, 7–8

Bellows, J., 11–12
Boke, K., 11, 16
Burke, T., 4–5, 19; dispatcher stress, 4–5

Castle, T., 4, 11, 18, 22–23, 65; jail officers, 4
chain of custody, 3, 8, 46
Childress, R., 4, 18–19, 21–22, 65
chronic stress (*See also* stress), 8, 23
Cold Case, 2, 25 (*See also* media, television dramas)
comparison to forensics on TV, 50 (*See also* media, television dramas)
Cooper, C., 18
Corbit, J., 13–14
Council on Forensic Science Education, 1
Court TV, 2, 25 (*See also* media, television dramas)
Coverdell Grants Program (*See* Paul Coverdell), 70
crime scene, 5–6, 8, 25, 43, 52, 71; responders, 6, 71
criminalist, 8, 32, 41, 43, 45–47

CSI, 1–2, 4–5, 8, 25–28, 42, 48, 50–51, 53–54, 60, 71 (*See also* media, television dramas)
"*CSI Effect*," 5, 8, 28, 48, 50, 53–54, 60, 71

Discrepancy Theory, 12–13, 63
DNA, 1, 3, 32, 41, 43, 45–46, 51–52, 58, 62; analysis, 1, 46; causing backlogs, 3; results, 41, 51–52
Dragnet, 24 (*See also* media, television dramas)

Eisner, M., 3, 11, 16, 22–23, 26, 65
epoche, 35, 48

Federal Bureau of Investigation (FBI), 1, 5
Finn, P., 17, 19, 21
forensic science, 1–8, 10–12, 14–15, 24–28, 31, 34, 37–39, 42, 44–47, 50–60, 63, 65–66, 68–71; definition, 24
forensic science personnel (dispatcher, scientist, crime scene responders, and others), 5–6, 15, 27
forensic scientists, 1–3, 5–9, 14, 24–28, 30, 32–37, 39, 41, 42, 44, 45, 48–65, 69–71
forensics on TV (*See* media, television dramas)

Galton, Francis, 25

Houck, Max, 3–4, 6, 25–26, 66
Husserl, E., 10

jail officers, 4
job aspects, 4
job–related stress, 22–23 (*See also* stress)
job satisfaction: reasons for lack of, 22

Kenny, D., 18
Kleck, G., 11–12

Landy, F., 11–14, 30, 63
Law & Order, 1–2, 5, 8, 25–26 (*See also* media, television dramas)
Lawler, E., 12–13, 63
Leedy, P., 8–10, 29, 31, 36, 38
Locard, E., 25
Locke, E., 11–12, 21, 62
Lyons, D., 3

Manzoni, P., 3, 11, 16, 22–23, 26, 65
media, 1–2, 5, 7–8, 16, 24–25, 34, 38, 44, 52–53, 55, 57–59, 62–63, 65–66, 69–70 (*See also* television dramas)
Moustakas, C., 10, 29, 35–37, 39, 41, 45, 47–50 (*See also* van Kaam Method)

Nalla, M., 11, 16
National Institute for Occupational Safety & Health (NIOSH), 16–17
National Research Council, 2, 4–5, 70
National Women's Health Resource Center (NWHRC), 17–18, 20, 23
NCIS, 25–26, 51 (*See also* media, television dramas)
Neuman, W., 7, 10, 29, 37

Opponent Process Theory, 12–14, 30, 39, 62–63
organizational stressors, 22 (*See also* stress)

Ormrod, J., 8–10, 29, 31, 36, 38
Osborn, A., 25

Paul Coverdell Forensic Science Improvement Grants Program, 70
phenomenological approach, 6, 10, 35
Phenomenology, 7, 10, 12, 29, 30, 39, 41; definition, 10

Quincy, ME, 24 (*See also* media, television dramas)

Sewell, J., 3–5, 11, 18–20, 22, 26, 28, 64–65, 69–70
Solomon, R., 13–14, 30
Sproull, N., 9, 31, 38–39, 56
stress, 1–8, 14–24, 26–28, 64, 65, 69; chronic, 8, 23; definition of, 17; reduction programs, 20–21; signs of, 17–18; symptoms of, 18; in workplace, 17, 21

Talucci, V., 4, 18–19
Tark, J., 11–12
television dramas (*See Cold Case, CSI, Dragnet, Law & Order, NCIS, Quincy ME*)
training (of forensic personnel), 2, 45–47, 55, 70

van Kaam (Adrian) Method, 37, 41, 47–50, 60–61 (*See also* Moustakas)

Wood, J., 4, 18–19
workplace, 7, 16–18, 20, 21, 23, 30, 62, 65, 68–70; negative variables of, 23, stress, 17, 21

ABOUT THE AUTHORS

Tharinia Dukes Robinson is a former Questioned Document Examiner with California Department of Justice Bureau of Forensic Services whose research interests include special topics in forensic science with primary emphasis on issues that affect the forensic scientist. Dukes Robinson is currently an assistant professor of criminal justice at Piedmont College in Demorest and Athens Georgia.

Ashraf Esmail is an independent scholar and researcher who serves as the senior editor for the *Journal of Education and Social Justice*. His research interests include: urban, multicultural, and peace education; family; cultural diversity; political sociology; criminology; social problems; and deviance.

www.ingramcontent.com/pod-product-compliance
Lightning Source LLC
Chambersburg PA
CBHW030909040526
R18240000002B/R182400PG44116CBX00003B/1